NOTES

including
- *Life of the Author*
- *List of Characters*
- *Chapter-by-Chapter Critical Commentaries*
- *Character Analyses*
- *Questions for Review*
- *Selected Bibliography*

by
Edward A. Kopper, Jr., Ph.D.
Professor of English
Slippery Rock State College

WILEY

Wiley Publishing, Inc.

Editor
Gary Carey, M.A., University of Colorado

Consulting Editor
James L. Roberts, Ph.D., Department of
English, University of Nebraska

Composition
Wiley Indianapolis Composition Services

CliffsNotes™ *Ulysses*

Published by:
Wiley Publishing, Inc.
111 River Street
Hoboken, NJ 07030-5774
www.wiley.com

CONTENTS

ULYSSES NOTES

LIFE OF THE AUTHOR

Born in Rathgar, a township of Dublin on February 2, 1882, James Joyce was the oldest of ten children, five others dying in infancy. Joyce's father, John Stanislaus Joyce (1849-1931), the prototype for Simon Dedalus of *Ulysses*, was a charming, bright, but improvident "Mr. Micawber" sort of man, one whose profligacy occasioned the ever-declining family fortunes and led the Joyce children to a life of impoverishment.

Despite his family's economic situation, however, Joyce did manage to secure a fine education. From 1888 to 1891, he attended the prestigious Clongowes Wood College in County Kildare, and, from 1893 to 1898, he attended the reputable Belvedere College, a Catholic day school in Dublin. Joyce graduated from University College, Dublin, in 1902.

One particularly important event that occurred during Joyce's schooldays was the death of Charles Stewart Parnell in October, 1891. The young Joyce, reinforced in his political and nationalistic convictions by his father, felt that the great nationalist leader, who fell from grace because of his affair with Kitty O'Shea, had been "betrayed" by his followers – that is, Parnell had been forced to resign from his position as head of Ireland's nationalist party because of the divorce trial of Captain and Kitty O'Shea. To commemorate the occasion of Parnell's death, the nine-year-old Joyce wrote a poem "Et Tu, Healy," which denounced the worst of the turncoats, and one reason that Stephen Dedalus in *A Portrait of the Artist as a Young Man* cites for leaving Ireland is his fear that the country will always destroy its prophets.

At University College, Dublin, Joyce openly espoused a number of unpopular causes. He insisted upon the worth of Henrik Ibsen, considered anathema by conservative Dublin Catholics, and, at the age of eighteen, he published an article on "Ibsen's New Drama" in the *Fortnightly Review*. In 1900, he delivered a paper, "Drama and Life," before the Literary and Historical Society of the College, which advocated modern dramatists, as opposed to Shakespeare and the Greeks. Joyce's article "The Day of the Rabblement" (1901) denounced the beginning Irish theater movement, which Joyce believed was too insular, too cut off from European culture. Lady Gregory, William Butler Yeats, and other leaders of the Irish Literary Theatre, it seemed to Joyce, were being too provincial in their stress upon peasant and folk drama.

After he left the University in 1902, Joyce went to Paris to study medicine and to write; after a brief time, he returned to Ireland, then left for Paris again in 1903 with the intention of devoting himself to full-time literary endeavors; he returned to Dublin when his father's telegram of April 10, 1903, announced his mother's imminent death (she died of cancer on August 13, 1903). Joyce's months of drifting in Dublin ended with the first days of 1904, when he seriously returned to his writing, and in June of that year, Joyce met Nora Barnacle, a twenty-year-old Galway woman, with whom he was to spend the rest of his life. The famous "Bloomsday" in *Ulysses*, June 16, is probably the day on which Joyce discovered that he was in love with Nora. In October, 1904, they left for Zurich, where Joyce had been promised a position teaching at the Berlitz School.

The period from October, 1904 (when Joyce arrived in Zurich to find that the administrators of the Berlitz School had never heard of his application), through the end of June, 1915 (when Joyce, because of World War I, decided to leave Trieste and to return to Zurich to take up residence), was a mixed one for Joyce. On the debit side one can place several items: Joyce's dislike of Pola, Rome, and Trieste, the last being his chief habitat during the years 1904-15; several years of delay in the publication of *Dubliners*, which was finally printed in 1914; a lie told to Joyce by his friend Vincent Cosgrave (in 1909, on a return visit to Ireland) concerning Nora's having been unfaithful during Joyce's courtship in 1904; and the failure, in 1909 in Dublin, of Joyce's venture into the cinema business, the Cinematograph Volta. Balanced against these disappointments, however, were the birth of his son, Giorgio, in 1905, and the birth of his daughter, Lucia Anna, in 1907; and the support of Yeats, Pound, and Dora Marsden, who agreed to publish *A Portrait of the Artist as a Young Man* in serial form in her review, *The Egoist*, between February 2, 1914, and September 1, 1915.

Joyce's financial situation improved considerably in Zurich. Through contacts, he tutored several language students, and, with the help of Pound and Yeats, he secured a grant from the Royal Literary Fund. Of greater importance, however, were two patronesses—Harriet Shaw Weaver, whose support of Joyce began in February, 1917, and Edith Rockefeller McCormick, an American living in Zurich, whose large stipend ran from March, 1918, through September, 1919. Miss Weaver, in addition, formed the Egoist Press to publish an English edition of *A Portrait*, in 1917, after B. W. Huebsch in New York had issued the novel in 1916. (Installments of *Ulysses* appeared in the *Little Review* in New York from March 1918 until September-December, 1920; and Joyce's play, *Exiles*, was published in 1918.)

With the improvement of his lifestyle, Joyce lost much of his bitterness towards the Ireland which he had decided never to visit again after 1912. In addition, in Zurich, he stepped up his "attack" upon the English language, his restructuring of traditional means of expression. Two clouds, however, did partially mar the relatively secure Zurich days: at the end of 1918 and the start of 1919, he began a tepid affair with a Swiss woman named Martha Fleischmann (she was Joyce's prototype for Martha Clifford in *Ulysses*), which ended sadly; and in August 1917, Joyce began undergoing the first of eleven eye operations that were to continue for fifteen years. He left Zurich for Trieste in October, 1919, and then, at Pound's urging, he decided in the late spring of 1920 to move to Paris, the city in which he was to spend the next nineteen years.

Joyce was relatively happy during his first years in the cosmopolitan city. Pound had arranged to have Joyce's books translated into French, and he felt that Paris was the best place to launch *Ulysses*. One friend lent Joyce a free flat; others, clothing and furniture. The well-known critic Valery Larbaud gave a public lecture on *Ulysses* two months before its publication, and the novel was finally published on Joyce's fortieth birthday, February 2, 1922, by Sylvia Beach's Shakespeare and Company.

On March 10, 1923, Joyce began *Finnegans Wake*, the book that was to appear in parts in several magazines (most prominently in Eugene and Maria Jolas's *transition* from April, 1927, to April-May, 1938) until its publication as a whole on May 4, 1939. This enigmatic book cost Joyce most of his old literary associates, and its seemingly meaningless language alienated many of his friends. Pound complained that he could not understand what Joyce was doing in his new work; as a result, Pound's relationship with Joyce was strained after the late 1920s. Joyce's brother Stanislaus judged the book to be drivel. Joyce himself was so discouraged with the reception of his new work that in 1929 he proposed to the Irish writer James Stephens that he finish the book for him. The timing of the publication of *Finnegans Wake* as a whole, just months short of the declaration of World War II, was the final blow to a broken Joyce, who, shortly after, was once again forced to move because of international hostilities. In addition to all of his other disappointments, Joyce spent the 1930s in a desperate attempt to cure the schizophrenia of his daughter, Lucia. The task was a hopeless one, but Joyce persisted in trying to effect a restoration.

Joyce died on January 13, 1941, as the result of an undiagnosed duodenal ulcer. He is buried in the Fluntern Cemetery, which rises above Zurich.

LIST OF CHARACTERS

Athos

A dog which belonged to Bloom's father, Rudolph. In his suicide note, the senior Bloom asked Bloom to care for the animal. Athos corresponds to Odysseus's Argos, the faithful dog who waited for his master's return; after Odysseus returned, the dog died.

Alec Bannon

Bannon, part of Buck Mulligan's circle, met Milly Bloom, Bloom's fifteen-year-old daughter, after Bloom sent her away to Mullingar to study photography in order to get her out of the house during the affair of Boylan and Molly. Bannon appears with Mulligan at Dr. Horne's hospital in "The Oxen of the Sun" and discusses Milly.

Philip Beaufoy

Beaufoy writes shoddy short stories for *Titbits*, and Bloom, thinking that Beaufoy is a fine writer, dreams of imitating him, especially his prize-winning "Matcham's Masterstroke."

Richard Irvine Best

Best was assistant director (and then director after 1904) of Dublin's National Library and appears in "Scylla and Charybdis."

A Blind Stripling

Bloom reveals his charitable nature in "The Lestrygonians" by helping this young man cross the street; later, the youth turns up as the blind piano tuner in "The Sirens." The stripling is bumped into by Lamppost Farrell in "The Wandering Rocks."

Leopold Bloom

Joyce's twentieth-century Odysseus-Ulysses figure; his wife is Molly, and he is an ad canvasser for the *Freeman's Journal*. For further discussion, see Character Analyses.

Marcus J. Bloom

This Bloom is the dental surgeon mentioned in "The Wandering Rocks." He is no relation to the protagonist, and his name provides one of the "traps" in the episode.

Milly Bloom

Bloom's fifteen-year-old daughter (See **Alec Bannon**); she is attractive, as is her mother, and she is apparently also a bit hefty. Although she is dating Bannon, she has not yet lost her virginity, even though her mother is "corrupted" by Boylan on June 16. Milly is a feisty lass, and often Molly has had to curb her insolence. Bloom's thoughts of Milly emphasize his stress concerning the passing of time: Milly is experiencing her first love at approximately the same age as Molly experienced hers, with Lieutenant Mulvey on Gibraltar.

Molly Bloom

Joyce's earth goddess, she is similar to Chaucer's Wife of Bath. Although her appearance in *Ulysses* occupies only a small part of the novel, her presence is felt throughout. For further discussion, see Character Analyses.

Rudolph Bloom

Bloom's father, born Rudolph Virag sometime between 1807 and 1816; he died in 1886. Bloom's planned trip to Ennis to commemorate the anniversary of his father's death will prevent him from being with Boylan and Molly during the upcoming concert tour to Belfast. Rudolph became despondent after his wife's death and finally poisoned himself.

Rudy Bloom

Bloom's son, who was born December 29, 1893, and who died January 9, 1894. Molly and Bloom have not had complete sexual intercourse since Rudy's death, and Rudy is indeed the last of the Virag-Bloom line. Rudy appears in a vision to Bloom at the end of "Circe" at the age he would have been had he lived.

Señor A. Boudin

Possibly the true name of the swaggering sailor W. B. Murphy, who appears in "Eumaeus."

Blazes Boylan

He is a singer, the owner of a prize fighter, and a "bill sticker"; Boylan has sex with Molly sometime shortly after 4:00 P.M. on June 16, 1904. For further discussion, see Character Analyses.

Denis Breen

Husband of Josie Breen, a half-mad eccentric who has received a postcard with "U.P.: up" written on it; he spends a good deal of time trying to find the lawyer Menton in order to file a lawsuit against the unknown jokester. Breen is ridiculed in "The Cyclops" as he passes Barney Kiernan's pub.

Davy Byrne

He runs a "moral" pub, to which Bloom escapes in "The Lestrygonians" to have a glass of burgundy and a cheese sandwich after he has left the swinish eaters at the restaurant of the Burton Hotel. He and Nosey Flynn think of Bloom as a decent, quiet man.

Cissy Caffrey

Gerty MacDowell's friend in "Nausicaa," who abets Gerty in the "seduction" of Bloom.

Private Harry Carr

He taunts Stephen at the beginning of "Circe" and then knocks him down near the end of that episode when he lets himself believe that Stephen is threatening the king. His companion is Private Compton.

The Citizen

This gross, ardently nationalistic anti-Semite, who can see reality with only one eye, is Joyce's modern-day equivalent of a cyclops. He throws a biscuit tin at Bloom at the end of "The Cyclops" as Bloom escapes in a "chariot" and ascends into "heaven." The Citizen is based on Michael ("Citizen") Cusack (1847-1907), whose purpose in life was to revive Gaelic games in Ireland.

Martha Clifford

Bloom's pen pal and platonic lover, with whom he corresponds under the pseudonym Henry Flower. Martha is one of at least forty-four respondents to Bloom's ad: "Wanted smart lady typist to aid gentleman in literary work." She is one of the mysteries in *Ulysses* since her name is undoubtedly false.

Mrs. Clinch

A respectable woman whom Bloom once almost accosted, thinking that she was a prostitute.

Cochrane

An inattentive student whom Stephen calls on at the start of his class in Mr. Deasy's school in "Nestor."

Father Francis Coffey

He performs the Absolution during the burial service of Paddy Dignam in Glasnevin Cemetery in "Hades." He corresponds to

Cerberus, the mythical dog that guards the entrance to Hell, or Hades.

Bella Cohen

Joyce's parallel to Homer's Circe, who turns men into swine. She tries to cheat Stephen during the Nighttown Episode, but Bloom saves Stephen's money by threatening to reveal that Bella is financing her son's way through Oxford by her earnings from prostitution. Bella becomes Bello (masculine) during Bloom's major masochistic "hallucination" in "Circe."

Father John Conmee, S. J.

The rector of Clongowes Wood College who saved Stephen from a beating in *A Portrait of the Artist as a Young Man*; he appears in "The Wandering Rocks," when he reminisces about his days at Clongowes.

John Corley

From "Two Gallants" in *Dubliners*. Corley sponges money from Stephen as Stephen and Bloom are heading for the cabman's shelter in "Eumaeus."

"Father" Bob Cowley

A spoiled priest, "Father" Cowley is one of the illusions in "The Wandering Rocks" since he is called by his first name, Bob, an odd appellation for a priest.

Cranly

Stephen's close friend in Book Five of *A Portrait of the Artist as a Young Man*. In that novel, he serves a role similar to Buck Mulligan's in *Ulysses*.

Myles Crawford

Editor of the *Evening Telegraph*; he rejects the compromise made between Bloom and Alexander Keyes over the ad for the House of Keyes (Keys), and his blithe (and drunken) attitude costs Bloom his main monetary gain of June 16.

J. T. A. Crofton

From "Ivy Day in the Committee Room" in *Dubliners*. At the end of "The Cyclops," he escapes from the Citizen-Cyclops along with Bloom, Martin Cunningham, and Jack Power in Cunningham's carriage.

Martin Cunningham

A sometimes kindly man who, on the way to Glasnevin Cemetery, tries to steer the conversation away from suicides (See Bloom's father). After leaving Barney Kiernan's in "The Cyclops," he and Bloom go to the Dignams' house to discuss Paddy's insurance with his widow.

Dan Dawson

His speech sentimentalizing Ireland as a land of purling rills is soundly ridiculed in "Aeolus."

Mr. Garrett Deasy

Headmaster of the school in Dalkey, where Stephen teaches; Deasy is anti-Semitic, stingy, anti-female, and pro-British. He corresponds to Nestor, the windbag orator of Homer's *Odyssey*.

Boody Dedalus

Stephen's starving sister who calls her father, Simon, "Our father who art not in heaven."

Dilly Dedalus

In a pathetic attempt to extricate herself from the family squalor, this sister of Stephen's buys a copy of *Chardenal's French Primer*. Bloom sees her as a poor, hungry child who stands outside auction rooms while her father is drinking in pubs.

Maggy Dedalus

Another impoverished sister of Stephen; she fails to convince a pawn shop to accept her brother's books.

Mrs. May (Mary) Dedalus

Stephen's refusal to pray at his mother's deathbed occasions his major guilt in *Ulysses*. His mother appears to him in "Circe," begging him to repent and to return to the Church. In an act of rebellion, Stephen smashes the brothel chandelier with his ashplant (walking stick) in "Circe."

Simon Dedalus

Stephen's alcoholic father; he counters neglect of his family with a fine sense of humor, a clear critical eye, and an excellent singing voice.

Stephen Dedalus

Joyce's bright, creative, but perplexed young hero, whose story begins in *A Portrait of the Artist as a Young Man*. For further discussion, see Character Analyses.

Charles-Paul de Kock

French novelist (1794-1871) who wrote trashy books for the lower-middle class. Molly thinks that he probably acquired his name because of his sexual proclivities.

Paddy (Patrick) Dignam

His death is the reason why Bloom is at Glasnevin Cemetery ("Hades") and the reason why Bloom is dressed in black throughout the day. Another drunken Dubliner, Dignam corresponds to Odysseus's inebriated retainer, Elpenor, who, in Homer's epic, broke his neck in a fall from the roof of Circe's house.

Master Patrick Dignam

The main interest of Dignam's son in his father's death is that he might get some time off from school and can become a celebrity for awhile.

Mat Dillon

His home provided a meeting place for Bloom and Molly in 1887 when they were going together. Also, it was at Dillon's that Bloom bested Menton at bowls, an affront that the solicitor never forgot.

Dr. Dixon

On May 23, 1904, Dixon treated Bloom for a bee sting, this wound in the side becoming a Christocentric symbol in *Ulysses.*

Moses Dlugacz

At the shop of this pork butcher, Bloom (in "Calypso") buys a kidney for breakfast. Also, at Dlugacz's, Bloom ogles the buxom servant girl of the Blooms' next door neighbors, the Woods, although he is unable to follow her after she leaves the store.

Reuben J. Dodd

A stingy legal accountant who is the butt of a joke among Cunningham, Power, Simon Dedalus, and Bloom on the way to Glasnevin Cemetery.

Ben Dollard

An overweight singer who gives a rendition of the patriotic ballad "The Croppy Boy" in "The Sirens." Molly once punned on Dollard's size, saying that he had a nice "barreltone" voice.

Bob Doran

From "The Boarding House" in *Dubliners.* Doran is on his annual drinking binge in *Ulysses,* and his sinister, drunken antics in "The Cyclops" help to establish the macabre tone of the episode.

Lydia Douce

One of Joyce's sirens in "The Sirens," Lydia Douce is a barmaid at the Ormond Hotel. Her observation that Bloom has "greasy eyes" relates him to Christ since the word is pronounced "grace-y" in Dublin. The other siren at the Ormond is Mina Kennedy.

Mary Driscoll

A maid at the Blooms' whom Molly dismissed on a false charge when Bloom began taking an interest in her.

Earl of Dudley (William Humble Ward)

The cavalcade of this Lord Lieutenant of Ireland to open the Mirus Bazaar is one of the structuring devices of "The Wandering Rocks."

Kevin Egan

A self-exiled Irish patriot whom Stephen meets in Paris before the start of *Ulysses*.

John Eglinton (William Kirkpatrick Magee)

Influential Anglo-Irish essayist who patronizes Stephen during Stephen's discussion of Shakespeare in "Scylla and Charybdis."

Lamppost (Cashel Boyle O'Connor Fitzmaurice Tisdall) Farrell

A Dublin eccentric known for his wild clothes and for his habit of walking outside of lampposts. Farrell is sitting in the National Library's reading room during the discussion of Shakespeare in "Scylla and Charybdis."

James (Skin-the-Goat) Fitzharris

He drove the decoy car after the Phoenix Park Assassinations of 1882. The cabman's shelter to which Bloom and Stephen go in "Eumaeus" is said to be operated by him (but probably is not).

"Henry Flower"

Bloom's alias in his correspondence with Martha Clifford.

Nosey Flynn

From "Counterparts" in *Dubliners*. A frequenter of Davy Byrne's, who praises Bloom in "The Lestrygonians."

Ignatius Gallaher

From "A Little Cloud" in *Dubliners*. The star reporter discussed in the newspaper offices in "Aeolus," Gallaher broke the story of the Phoenix Park Assassinations, possibly (Joyce implies) by infiltrating the group of Irish extremists.

Lieutenant Stanley G. Gardner

Discussed in "Penelope," Gardner is probably the only person (besides Bloom and Boylan) who has complete sexual intercourse with Molly during her marriage. If the affair did take place, it happened between 1899 and 1901. Gardner died of fever in South Africa during the Boer War.

Garryowen

The large dog that menaces Bloom in Barney Kiernan's pub in "The Cyclops." It belongs to Gerty MacDowell's grandfather, Giltrap.

Uncle Richie Goulding

Stephen's uncle, whom he considers visiting in "Proteus." Simon Dedalus intensely dislikes his brother-in-law, who has been ruined by drink and who forms a pathetic figure as he eats with Bloom (another outcast) in "The Sirens."

Haines

The patronizing, anti-Semitic Oxonian who rooms with Mulligan and Stephen in the Martello Tower. Haines, who has come to Ireland to study Irish folklore, simplistically asserts that all of Ireland's troubles are attributable to "history," not to British misuse.

Charles Wisdom Hely

The Dublin stationer and printer for whom Bloom used to work. Men advertising his business appear in "The Lestrygonians," walking about wearing scarlet letters on large white hats.

Ellen Higgins

Bloom's mother, who married Rudolph Bloom, about 1865.

Zoe Higgins

A prostitute in "Circe" who takes away Bloom's talisman, a potato, which corresponds to Odysseus's *moly* (the herb that prevented Odysseus from being turned into a swine by Circe).

Dr. Andrew J. Horne

One of the superintendents of Dublin's National Maternity Hospital, the setting for "The Oxen of the Sun."

Joe Hynes

From "Ivy Day in the Committee Room" in *Dubliners*. Vaguely associated with the *Freeman's Journal* and the *Evening Telegraph*, Hynes unwittingly includes several bits of false information in his report of Paddy Dignam's funeral. Although Hynes owes Bloom money (for which Bloom has asked him three times), Hynes appears in "The Cyclops" and buys drinks for himself and others.

Georgina Johnson

A prostitute upon whom Stephen spent the pound that he had borrowed from George Russell (A.E.). The loan is the basis for the execrable pun on Russell's appellation: "A.E.I.O.U."

Kathleen Kearney

From "A Mother" in *Dubliners*. A rising songstress of whom lly is jealous.

Corny Kelleher

Works for an undertaker and is rumored to have underworld connections. In "The Wandering Rocks," Kelleher spits out a "silent jet of hayjuice," and in "Circe," he refuses to take Stephen home after Private Carr has knocked him down.

Alexander Keyes

The tea merchant with whom Bloom negotiates the placing of an ad in the *Freeman's Journal*. Keyes will grant a two-month renewal of the ad in exchange for a free paragraph "puffing" his establishment in *Freeman's*. Myles Crawford, the editor, insists on three months, and Bloom is caught in the middle.

Barney Kiernan

The Cyclops Episode takes place in his pub and begins just before 5:00 P.M.

"Kinch"

Stephen's nickname; the sound of the word is probably suggestive of the cutting sound made by a knife, a reference to Stephen's sharp Aristotelian logic.

Ned Lambert

One of the discussants at the *Freeman's* office during "Aeolus." He and Simon Dedalus leave the others for a drink at The Oval.

Lunita Laredo

Molly's mother, who married Major Brian Cooper Tweedy. She was a Spanish Jewess and probably somewhat "fast." There are hints in *Ulysses* that Lunita and Tweedy were not really married and that Molly thus may be illegitimate (another mystery in the novel).

T. Lenehan

From "Two Gallants." Lenehan apologizes with exaggerated politeness when he collides with Bloom in the *Freeman's* offices, helps spread the rumor that Bloom is betting on Throwaway in the Ascot Gold Cup race, and is "put down" by M'Coy (in "The Wandering Rocks") when he (Lenehan) boasts of once taking liberties with Molly.

Vincent Lynch

A friend of Stephen's who accompanies him to Nighttown in "Circe" and later deserts him in the brothel area. Lynch is a Judas figure in *Ulysses*.

Bantam Lyons

From "Ivy Day in the Committee Room." Spreads the false information that Bloom has bet on the horse Throwaway when (in "The Lotus-Eaters") Bloom tells him that he is going to throw away his copy of the *Freeman's Journal* and that Lyons can have it. Lyons passes the false tip to Davy Byrne and Nosey Flynn in "The Lestrygonians" and later to Lenehan.

Thomas William Lyster

The "Quaker Librarian" who appears in the National Library in "Scylla and Charybdis" and discusses aesthetics with Stephen and others.

Florence MacCabe

An old woman whom Stephen sees on the beach in "Proteus"; probably the same Florence MacCabe who figures in Stephen's Parable of the Plums. In both cases, Stephen *calls* the woman this name.

Gerty MacDowell

Joyce's Nausicaa, who entices Bloom into masturbating when she reveals her upper thigh and underwear in Joyce's thirteenth episode.

Professor Hugh MacHugh

One of the principals in the newspaper offices in "Aeolus," MacHugh underlines the theme of Ireland's bondage to Britain.

Man in the Macintosh

A mysterious figure who turns up at Dignam's funeral. Hynes, mishearing a remark by Bloom in "Hades," has him appear as a person named M'Intosh in the *Telegraph* article.

Mrs. Mastiansky

A friend of Molly's. In "Penelope," Molly alludes to the unusual sexual practices of Mr. Mastiansky.

C. P. M'Coy

A strange Dubliner who is in the habit of borrowing valises and then pawning them. Although he does not show up at Dignam's funeral, he is reported to have been there in Hynes's newspaper story.

John Henry Menton

A solicitor who is ruffled in "Hades" when Bloom points out a dent in his hat. Menton was once a rival for Molly's affections, and, in 1887, at Mat Dillon's, Bloom bested him at a game of bowls.

George Robert Mesias

Bloom's tailor who once explained that Bloom was hard to fit since both his testicles were on the right side. Bloom became acquainted with Boylan at Mesias's shop in September, 1903.

George Moore

Well-known Irish novelist. It is revealed in "Scylla and Charybdis" that Stephen has not been invited to Moore's get-together on the evening of June 16, even though Mulligan and Haines have been asked to come to the literary discussion.

Buck Mulligan

The complex alter ego of Stephen; he is witty, cynical, and blasphemous, but he is also courageous. Mulligan "baits" Stephen several times in *Ulysses* and, finally, he apparently has a physical scuffle with him before Stephen leaves for the brothel district. At the end of *Ulysses*, Mulligan and Haines return to the Martello Tower, and the now homeless Stephen finds that his place has been irrevocably usurped by this Dublin medical student.

Lieutenant Harry Mulvey

Molly's first love, when she was fifteen, on Gibraltar. In "Penelope," Molly remembers masturbating him into a handkerchief, and she wonders what he is doing now.

W. B. Murphy

A sailor who appears in the cabman's shelter in "Eumaeus"; the drunken red-bearded Murphy is Joyce's embodiment of the Returning Wanderer. He is apparently from the three-master *Rosevean*, which Stephen sees at the end of "Proteus."

Joseph Patrick Nannetti

Foreman of the *Freeman's* who half-listens to Bloom's problems over the Keyes's ad, then leaves Dublin for the House of Commons, having settled nothing about the exchange.

J. J. O'Molloy

One of the cronies at the newspaper office in "Aeolus." He opens a door and strikes Bloom (accidently); there is no room for Bloom in this "inn."

Charles Stewart Parnell

The great Irish nationalist whose fall influenced so much of *A Portrait of the Artist as a Young Man* and *Ulysses*. Parnell's demise began in 1890, when details of his relationship with Kitty O'Shea, his mistress, were revealed in the O'Shea divorce trial. He died in 1891. Myths surrounding Parnell are discussed most prominently in "Eumaeus."

Pat the Waiter

In "The Sirens," Pat is described as being "a waiter who waits while you wait." At this point, Bloom too is "waiting" – for the adultery of Boylan and Molly to begin.

Jack Power

His unknowing comments about suicides on the way to Dignam's funeral embarrass Bloom, although Martin Cunningham tries to console him. Later, Bloom meets with Cunningham, Power, and Crofton in Barney Kiernan's pub ("The Cyclops").

Mina Purefoy

Mrs. "Purefaith" has lain three days in labor, and her new son is finally born in "The Oxen of the Sun." Her husband's name is Theodore ("God-given").

Mrs. "Dante" Riordan

Stephen's tutor in *A Portrait of the Artist as a Young Man*; she is also a friend of the Blooms. Molly ridicules her in "Penelope" because Mrs. Riordan didn't leave them a bequest.

Harry Rumbold

A barber-hangman whose application for the post of executioner is discussed at length in "The Cyclops."

George Russell (A. E.)

Theosophist and man of letters whose stress upon the essences and ultimate forms of things in his discussion of Shakespeare in "Scylla and Charybdis" casts him as "Plato," in contrast to Stephen, who is "Aristotle." Bloom sees Russell bicycling in "The Lestrygonians," accompanied by Lizzie Twigg, the young woman whom Bloom rejected for the typist position in favor of Martha Clifford.

Cyril Sargent

A sniveling student in Stephen's class at Mr. Deasy's school, who (because of his ineptitude) reminds Stephen of his own school days at Clongowes.

Sceptre

The horse which Boylan bets on that loses the Gold Cup race. See **Throwaway**.

The Shan Van Vocht

The Poor Old Woman who personifies downtrodden Ireland, but who will become a beautiful queen when the country takes its rightful place in the world. Joyce's parody of this mythic creature is embodied in this old lady who brings milk to the Martello Tower in "Telemachus."

F. W. Sweny

The druggist from whom Bloom buys a bar of lemon soap, but Bloom forgets to return to the druggist's shop to pick up Molly's skin lotion.

Talbot

A cheating student in Stephen's class at Deasy's school.

Tatters

A dog which Stephen sees on the beach in "Proteus"; Stephen wonders if the animal is digging up his (the dog's) grandmother. Tatters typifies the "God-dog" theme in *Ulysses*.

John F. Taylor

A famous Dublin orator whose speech of October 24, 1901, in favor of reviving Gaelic is praised in "Aeolus."

Throwaway

The dark horse who wins the 1904 Gold Cup race, besting Sceptre, Boylan's choice. Like Throwaway, Bloom has been "thrown away" by Molly, but he may yet end by winning over Boylan. It is the mistaken belief that Bloom has won on the race that causes him trouble in "The Cyclops," when the men at Barney Kiernan's pub wonder why Bloom won't stand them to drinks to celebrate his gains. See **Bantam Lyons**.

Major Brian Cooper Tweedy

Molly's hard-drinking, pipe-smoking father, who was stationed on Gibraltar when she was born. Whether or not Tweedy was a major at all and not just a sergeant-major, and whether or not he is indeed Molly's father through a union with Lunita Laredo are two of the mysteries of *Ulysses*.

Lizzie Twigg

Applicant for the job of typist in response to Bloom's ad, whom Bloom turns down because he thinks she might be too arty. Twigg was an actual poetess and an associate of George Russell (A. E.).

Virag

The name of Bloom's father, grandfather, and great grandfather. Bloom's father changed his name to "Bloom," from "Virag," which means "flower" in Hungarian.

Reggie Wylie

Gerty MacDowell's boyfriend, with whom she has had a spat, probably making her more enthusiastic about "seducing" Bloom in "Nausicaa."

CRITICAL COMMENTARIES

Chapter 1:   Telemachus*

At about eight o'clock in the morning of June 16, 1904, on the stairhead of the Martello Tower on the beach bordering Dublin Bay at Sandycove, about seven miles south of Dublin, Stephen Dedalus has just awakened. He is living in the Tower (which he rented from the government) with Buck Mulligan, a Dublin medical student, and with Haines, an Oxonian, who is residing in Ireland while studying Irish folklore. Stephen is about to leave the Tower, and Joyce will liken Stephen's leaving to that of Homer's Telemachus, the son of the Greek hero Odysseus (Ulysses). Parallels with the Greek *Odyssey* are loose throughout Joyce's novel, but they serve as structuring devices which permit Joyce to carry through his mock heroic purpose in *Ulysses*. In the *Odyssey*, Telemachus decides to leave Ithaca to seek his long-lost father so that he and Odysseus (Ulysses) might return to drive away the suitors who are despoiling the kingdom while courting Penelope. In "Telemachus," Stephen Dedalus feels that he is being forced out of the Tower by Haines and Mulligan; and, in the last word of the chapter, he sees Mulligan as a "usurper."

Some important differences, however, emerge between Joyce's *Ulysses* and the *Odyssey*. Stephen does not leave the Martello Tower with the intention of searching for a father, even though his thoughts are about paternity, both physical and spiritual, and he voluntarily surrenders the key to the Tower to Mulligan. Also, his purpose is less firm than is that of Telemachus; when Stephen leaves Sandycove at the end of the episode, he has decided not to return to the Tower, but it is only after an argument late that night with Mulligan at the Westland Row Station, in which he almost certainly came to blows, that Stephen realizes the impossibility of going back. When Mulligan

---

* Joyce, of course, did not divide the novel into numbered or titled chapters, but for the sake of reference and clarity, these Commentaries have been labeled according to the standard divisions of Stuart Gilbert.

deserts him, Stephen ends up in the brothel district at midnight, shepherded by Bloom.

Central to this chapter is the contrast between Mulligan and Stephen: the cynic vs. the idealist, the scientist vs. the artist, and the robust extrovert vs. the contemplative introvert. Buck offers Stephen the temptation of an enjoyably physical but conventional existence, but Stephen treads deftly between such a life and its opposite, a labyrinthine maze of self-doubt, self-examination, and unhappiness. For example, Stephen is a nonbeliever in traditional Catholicism, but he is unable to tolerate Mulligan's blaspheming lifestyle, although in many ways it is attractive to him.

From the start of *Ulysses*, Mulligan's treatment of Stephen is brutal. He speaks to Stephen "coarsely," he ridicules Stephen's Greek name, and he reminds Stephen constantly of his refusal to pray at the bedside of his dying mother (who died a little less than a year before the opening of *Ulysses*); thus Mulligan augments the guilt from which Stephen suffers throughout the novel. In addition, Mulligan takes Stephen's money without qualm; while patronizing the old milk woman (whom he feels superior to), Mulligan says that if Irish people drank such good beverages regularly, they wouldn't have rotten teeth—which Stephen has. In contrast, Mulligan's teeth are solidly white and gold edged; he chides Stephen further for not washing frequently, while he, Mulligan, enjoys diving into the cold sea, and once he even saved a person from drowning (Stephen, metaphorically, could not even save his own mother from "drowning"). Mulligan also scolds Stephen for querulously discussing money in front of Haines, although he himself dislikes the bland Englishman and although he himself is unable to pay the old milk woman's entire bill.

In contrast to Mulligan, who can think of little else than the immediate future—that is, sharing Stephen's pay-day salary for drinks at The Ship pub—Stephen is mired in the past, chained to memories of his mother's death. It is not until Stephen smashes the symbolic chandelier in the brothel in "Circe" that he begins to take a small, first step to rid himself of his obsession with the past. The details of Mary Dedalus's death, both in Stephen's recurrent dream and in actuality, are indeed horrible and naturalistic, but they are balanced against such delicate pictures as Stephen's singing William Butler Yeats's "Who Goes with Fergus?" to his mother on her deathbed and also with his memory of how much his mother enjoyed, long ago, the Dublin version of Turko the Terrible's pantomime.

To emphasize Stephen's inward turnings, Joyce brilliantly explores one detail about Stephen, which he withholds from the reader until the "Circe" chapter: Stephen broke his glasses on June 15, and on this climactic day of June 16, he cannot see very well—particularly, physically. Besides reinforcing the role of Stephen as a visionary and as a "blind prophet," in contrast to the outer-oriented Mulligan, Stephen's myopia continues as a motif from Joyce's earlier novel (also dealing with Stephen), *A Portrait of the Artist as a Young Man*, in which, while a small boy at Clongowes Wood College, Stephen was unjustly punished by the clergy after he accidentally broke his spectacles. In the earlier novel, Stephen's physical near-blindness helped him to gain inner vision—that is, it assisted him to ultimately break from traditional Catholicism.

Yet before we can completely grasp the contrast between the two youths and fully comprehend Mulligan's deprecating treatment of Stephen before, during, and after breakfast, we must be aware of some facts about Catholicism, Joyce's personal background, and Irish history (the nightmare from which Stephen is trying to awaken).

To do this, we should be aware of several motifs that are developed throughout *Ulysses*. Some of the more important of these are religious symbols: the lost (and also the false) father theme, the image of Ireland as a desiccated wasteland, seen in the visit of the old milk woman, and the image of the key. These motifs are often blended, and one must never forget that *Ulysses* is a vast symphony of symbols and recurring images.

Most of the religious symbols are clearly and easily discernible. As examples, consider Mulligan's role as a false priest; *Malachi* Mulligan's shaving bowl is a chalice, and his quotation from the Introit ("*Introibo ad altare Dei*"—"I will go to the altar of God"), spoken from atop the stairs, suggests the traditional Catholic Mass (common to Joyce's day), in which the celebrant ascends a number of steps at the beginning of the service; here, Joyce assigns the role of a high priest to the Jewish Malachi, and thus Mulligan metaphorically places Stephen in the inferior position of an acolyte; the allusion shortly afterwards to "Christine" again suggests the Eucharistic ceremony.

The religious imagery surrounding Mulligan suggests, also, that even this liberated medical student, for all his profanity, cannot rid himself of his theological training. For instance, the appearance of the Catholic priest near Mulligan's forty-foot "swimming hole," besides implying the ubiquitousness of the clergy in Ireland, implies that Buck's immersion into the waters of joyful paganism can result in only a partial cleansing from his Irish Catholicism.

Other religious allusions, however, are more subtle. Mulligan's gesture of turning his shaven cheek over his shoulder to speak to Stephen resembles the gesticulations of a priest at the altar during Mass, when celebrants officiated with their backs to the acolytes and the congregation. Mulligan calls Stephen "poor dogsbody," foreshadowing an important confrontation with an actual dog in "Proteus" and reminding the reader of the famous Joycean adage that *God* is *dog* spelled backwards. Stephen's reference to himself as a "server of a servant" spells out his relationship to Ireland, a country which is itself a servant to two foreign tyrants, England and Rome; and it also suggests one of the Pope's titles, "Server of the Servants of God," and thus is part of the mock heroic tone of *Ulysses*. Consider also the old milk woman's "Glory be to God"; it is the start of an ironic Gloria, another prayer used in masses during certain joyful times of the year.

Religious allusions are used, as well, to express the false father theme of *Ulysses*. Haines has nightmares about being attacked by a black panther, and one apocryphal tradition holds that Christ's father was a Roman centurion named Panther or Pantherus (Joyce uses this legend in *Finnegans Wake*). Mulligan recites his irreverent "Ballad of Joking Jesus," with its parody of the Virgin birth ("My mother's a jew, my father's a bird"), after he has flung his towel around his neck as if it were a priest's stole ("stolewise"). In a similar vein, the heretics Arius and Sabellius long ago debated the procession, or order, of the members of the Trinity.

Stephen is clearly alienated from Mulligan; he is also condemned to remain apart from Haines, whom he dislikes. Haines has been to a good school, Oxford; Joyce (if we read *Ulysses* autobiographically) resented the fact that he was forced to attend University College, Dublin, which he considered inferior to Trinity College (Dublin), which has reciprocity with Oxford and Cambridge. Haines has money; the Dedalus family lives in dire poverty. Haines is part of the British tennis set. He is also a bit of a fascist—an anti-Semite who, in addition, excuses England's barbarous treatment of the Irish througout history. Added to these problems for Stephen is the irony that he is being virtually forced out of a place for which *he* – not Mulligan – pays the rent, and, in addition, he is still brooding over his part in his mother's unhappiness on her deathbed. What nightly surcease from his difficulties which Stephen might find is hampered by Haines's noisy nightmares, a situation which occasions Stephen's ultimatum to Mulligan about Haines's having to leave.

The false father theme is reinforced in this chapter by the many references to Shakespeare, especially to *Hamlet,* and these are developed at length in "Scylla and Charybdis." Already in "Telemachus," Stephen emerges as a Hamlet figure, and Mulligan as a false Horatio. Symbolically, the top of the Martello Tower becomes the heights of Elsinor, and both overlook abysses of figurative madness that both Hamlet and Stephen are facing.

After Mulligan's shave (Stephen himself detests washing and water generally), after breakfast, and after the visit of the old milk woman, the three young men go outside of the Martello Tower: Mulligan takes his plunge into the water, Haines sits on a rock watching him, and Stephen (taking up his "prophetic" ashplant) begins to walk along a path. Stephen, half in pique and half in despair, has surrendered the key to the Tower to the usurper Mulligan, and Stephen is now both symbolically and literally homeless. He has been victimized by the tyrant Mulligan, just as his country has been spiritually "usurped" and plundered by England (Haines).

Clearly, the emptiness of Irish Catholicism and the desperate lack of clear ideals and leaders are joined with Joyce's depiction of the futility of the Irish Renaissance, a literary movement which turned for inspiration and subject matter to the country's roots, here personified in the arid old milkwoman. The old lady is a parody of the Shan van Vocht, the Poor Old Lady of Irish lore, who will turn into a beautiful young queen when Ireland begins to take her place among the nations of the world. Her most prominent appearance in Irish Renaissance literature is in Yeats's play *Cathleen ni Houlihan,* in which she arrives to inspire a young man to take up arms against the British during the Rebellion of 1798.

Joyce's symbolic Shan van Vocht, however, has little ability to inspire anyone. She delivers milk but, in her, the milk of life has dried up; she arrives late; she prefers the loud, posturing medicine man, Mulligan, to the withdrawn intellectual, Stephen. She is not bothered very much by the fact that an Englishman, Haines, can speak Gaelic while she cannot, and although she admits that she is ashamed of her deficiency, she accepts the judgment of those who can speak the tongue that Irish is a "grand language." By picturing the old milkwoman as a "witch on her toadstool," Joyce is excoriating the folklore excavations of such writers as Yeats and Lady Gregory, who went from cottage to cottage recording the tales of western Irelanders. Joyce, who looked to Europe for artistic inspiration, thought such renderings to be empty exercises, products of senile minds, inventing a false past to evade present responsibilities. This escapism is seen in the wretched life of Mary Dedalus, another victim of rote acceptance of the status quo, and Stephen cannot help but see the similarities between the old crone and his own mother.

In one sense, then, "Telemachus" asks the question: "Who will hold the key to Ireland's future?" Will it be Mulligan, who at the end of the chapter has the large key to the Martello Tower, using it to press down his clothing? Or will it be Bloom, who spends the entirety of the novel trying to negotiate an advertisement with the House of Keyes and who neglects, on the morning of June 16, to bring with him his own key to his house at 7 Eccles Street and must, in "Ithaca," find another way to get into his own home (like Homer's Odysseus)? Is the key to *Ulysses* to be found in the brash physicality of Mulligan, the solipsistic intellectuality of Stephen, or the passivity and humanitarianism of Bloom? Although Joyce never does answer these questions, the novel depicts and suggests many possibilities.

Chapter 2: Nestor

Chapter 2 takes place at Headmaster Garrett Deasy's school on Dalkey Avenue in Dalkey, about one mile southeast of the Martello Tower at Sandycove. Stephen would undoubtedly have walked the short distance and would have arrived just after nine o'clock, a bit tardily. His conservation with Mr. Deasy ends just before 10:30 A.M. The time of the Nestor Episode is traditionally set at 10:00 A.M. because this is the hour at which the boys break for their hockey practice, during Stephen's history lesson.

The chapter begins with Stephen's calling on Cochrane, a student whose lack of enthusiasm typifies the feelings of Stephen's unruly class, whose members would rather listen to their teacher's riddles and jokes (which they ridicule). The lesson is about the Greek hero

Pyrrhus, another victim of a usurper, who, like the archetypal Irish prophet, remained faithful to a lost cause to the end. After he dismisses the class, Stephen spends time helping the inept student Cyril Sargent; he realizes that the boy's mother must once have loved this tired child in spite of his inadequacies, and Stephen is reminded again of the loss of his mother, Mary Dedalus.

A short time later, in Mr. Deasy's study, Stephen listens to his headmaster's moralizing, then accepts his meager salary from Deasy. Mr. Deasy also gives Stephen a letter which he has written about the foot and mouth disease of livestock, cattle in particular. Stephen has friends among editors, and Deasy feels that there will be no trouble in getting his (cliche-filled) letter published in the newspaper.

In terms of the *Odyssey*, Mr. Deasy, the stuffy, Polonius-like administrator, represents Nestor, the aged Greek soldier and rhetorician who helped to keep order among the military principals during the ten-year siege of Troy (described in the *Iliad*) and who was the first friend of Odysseus that Telemachus visited after he left Ithaca in search of information about his father. In this chapter, several parallels between the two men are found. Nestor, though often useful at Troy, is frequently satirized by Homer because of his ponderous verbiage; and it is significant that Telemachus does not gain any valuable information about him. Mr. Deasy, too, may have some sense of national and civic pride, as seen in his concern for sick cattle, but his virtue is outweighed by his militant anti-Semitism, his veneration of money, and his bland interpretation of the place of Protestantism in Irish history. In addition, Nestor was well known as a charioteer and a tamer of horses, and this fact is mirrored in Deasy's horse-racing mementos, whose descriptions foreshadow Bloom's entanglement with the misinterpreted "tip" on the horse Throwaway.

Other obscure but useful and significant allusions to the original Nestor Episode in the *Odyssey* add to the irony of Joyce's *Ulysses*. The contemporary Nestor restores order on a hockey field, not on a battleground, and his men are children; although he is old (an explicit parallel with Nestor of the *Odyssey*), Deasy assures Stephen that he occasionally likes "to break a lance" (argue jestingly) with him; and at the conclusion of the chapter, the sun casts spangles on Deasy's shoulders, suggesting the shining armor of a retiring soldier.

But this chapter is really "about" history, the nightmare from which Stephen is trying to awaken, and the "history" here is personal as well as national and military. While Stephen is inattentively lecturing to his inattentive class, his thoughts remain fixated on the subject that occupied him in "Telemachus," the reason why he has vowed to wear black for a year: his mother's ghastly death. When the boys ask him to tell a ghost story (in the middle of the disorderly class period), he immediately thinks of Milton's *Lycidas*, a poem wherein Milton promised immortality for his drowned friend, Edward King. In the poem, there is much water imagery, and this idea continues the water motif that Joyce began in the first chapter, while blending in the image of green bile that Stephen constantly associates with Mary Dedalus's death.

Bound up in Stephen's "personal history" are his lingering belief in spirituality, his hope for Miltonic salvation for his mother (in spite of his refusal to pray at her deathbed), his memory (tinged with sarcasm) of holier times spent in the library of Saint Geneviere in Paris (protected from the free-living life of sin outside the library walls), and, especially, the riddle of the fox burying his grandmother under a hollybush. The "poor soul" whose time it is to "go to heaven" is Mrs. Dedalus, and a religious interpretation of the riddle finds support in the next chapter when Stephen wonders if the dog on the beach, Tatters, is digging in the sand for his grandmother. Just before starting to dig, Tatters sniffs the bloated carcass of a dead dog, which has already been associated with the dog-God symbolism of *Ulysses* by the expression "dogsbody" in "Telemachus."

Even in Stephen's interview with the sniveling Cyril Sargent, we realize how Stephen is doomed to relive the past, the real nightmare of history, and how the past always leads back to his mother. In Cyril, Stephen sees himself as he was at Clongowes: weak-eyed, insecure, misunderstood, trembling, and put upon by the school disciplinarian. But, Stephen reasons, Cyril's mother must have loved him, and this thought leads once again to a memory of the pervasive odor of "rosewood and wetted ashes" that accompanied Mrs. Dedalus's last days.

Stephen's problems have taken a toll on him, and Joyce implies a good deal about his young but tired protagonist by giving us a high selectivity of important details. For example, Stephen's class is not only unruly but is also filled with cheaters; even the teacher, he himself, "cheats," and, in fact, Stephen does not care if his students cheat or not. Stephen has to glance as his "gorescarred" book (Joyce's term for Stephen's military history book) to note the place, Asculum, of Pyrrhus's 279 B.C. victory against the Romans; and the student Talbot haltingly reads parts of *Lycidas* from a secreted text. Stephen is aware of Talbot's subterfuge, for he sarcastically tells him to "turn over" the page after Talbot inadvertently repeats the phrase "Through the dear might. . . ."

Talbot's failing ploy and Stephen's inflectionless response permit Joyce to imply the ironic question of which is more absurd: forcing children to mutilate a great work of art by memorization, or Milton's doctrine of immortality itself. The answer is found in the realization that Stephen's somber point of view is the center of this chapter: Mulligan might have laughed at the absurdity of the question (while tanning Talbot's rump), but Stephen can only wonder whether, in fact, Christ did walk on water. Mired in guilt and sorrow, Stephen cannot enjoy life. He knows, for example, that his pun about a pier, that it is a "disappointed bridge," is clever, but he can think only that, when he repeats it, Haines will simply place it among his collection of Stephen's "bright" sayings; once again Stephen will be labeled as merely a jester at the court of the English tyrant.

Stephen's "personal history," with its bitter internal struggles, is also a microcosm of all of human history, seen in this chapter to be a series of life-and-death battles, ranging from ancient Greece to modern Ireland. However, the allusions to Helen, Julius Caesar, and Pyrrhus, while they are significant in a mock heroic novel based upon ancient prototypes, are less important than the references to the more contemporary betrayal and imprisonment of Ireland by England. And the spokesman for the Establishment is Garrett Deasy, who is a true West Briton—that is, he is an Irishman who imitates English manners and takes the British position on all matters.

Joyce feels that Deasy's view of Irish history is so destructive that he turns over the second half of the chapter to him, letting Deasy condemn himself with his own words. Joyce also gains an excellent structural framework for this chapter by placing Deasy at the center of the stage. In the first half of the chapter, Stephen attempted to lecture to his unwilling and somewhat obstreperous students; now Deasy is the instructor and Stephen is his reluctant interlocutor, as he repeats the part of gadfly-acolyte that he played for the celebrant Mulligan in "Telemachus."

Deasy blames women for the evils of history, and his views are as specious as those of Haines, who, in "Telemachus," maintained timidly that history, not the English, was to blame for Ireland's troubles. Apart from Eve, who first introduced sin into the world, Deasy censures Helen of Troy; Dervorgilla (the wife of the twelfth-century O'Rourke, Prince of Breffni and East Meath); and Kitty O'Shea (the wife of Captain O'Shea and the mistress of Charles Stewart Parnell). Helen is humorously appropriate in the mock heroic *Ulysses* since Nestor, in the *Odyssey*, sent Telemachus to Menelaus and Helen when he was unable to tell Telemachus much about his father. The reference to Dervorgilla shows that Deasy is not a precise scholar of Irish history; MacMurrough was *not* her husband; he was the lover with whom she ran off, occasioning O'Rourke to call in the English to help and bring them to Ireland for the first time (they never left). And the allusion to Parnell, the "Uncrowned King of Ireland," recalls the great political trauma of James Joyce's youth: the betrayal of Parnell by his followers because of the scandal of Parnell's involvement with Mrs. O'Shea. Of greatest importance about the stories of these three faithless wives, however, is that all three are different versions of Molly Bloom, who, on June 16, 1904, with Blazes Boylan, will enjoy an act of adultery.

In much the same manner, Deasy's distorted view of Jews fore-shadows the treatment that Leopold Bloom will receive in *Ulysses* at the hands of predominantly Catholic Dubliners. Deasy feels that England is decaying because Jews are controlling the finances and the press. He sees them as "sinners against the light" in their unwillingness to acknowledge Christ as their Savior, and the image blends well with Bloom, who wears a black suit all day after attending the funeral of Paddy Dignam in "Hades." Deasy's description of Jews as being wanderers over the earth anticipates the role of Bloom as the Wandering Jew. And the crude joke that Deasy tells about Ireland's being the only country never to have persecuted the Jews (the Irish never let them in) establishes the scornful atmosphere that Bloom must wander in throughout the day.

Reinforcing the historical motif in "Nestor" is the theme of money and Joyce's insistence that excessive stress on monetary values has done much to destroy Ireland. Talk of money permeates the chapter, and one is reminded of the lines from Yeats's poem "September 1913": "For men were born to pray and save:/ Romantic Ireland's dead and gone,/ It's with O'Leary in the grave." In the double pun, modern prophets "prey" for forsaking salvation in order to "save" material things; and although in *Ulysses*, Deasy's play on words is unintentional, Joyce wants the reader to catch the irony of such an admonition's being directed at his mock heroic Christ figure, Stephen: "Because you don't save. . . ."

Deasy, then, is the spokesman for the world-as-finance. The insolence of the students at his school is occasioned by their parents' wealth; they contrast with Stephen, who was the "poor boy" at Clongowes, forced to make up stories about his parentage. To Deasy, virtue means never having to say you borrowed. Even Deasy's plan to cure foot and mouth disease by using Koch's preparation (the wrong antidote, but one which does suggest a favorite author of Molly Bloom, Charles-Paul de Kock) is meant to prevent an embargo on Irish cattle with its subsequent loss of revenue. It is no wonder that the last picture we have of Deasy is epitomized by the last word of the chapter: "coins."

"Nestor," then, besides being "about" Stephen's personal difficulties, concerns two great forces in human history: military conquest and greed. Joyce calls attention to his dual theme by having Stephen's lesson focus on Pyrrhus during history class and on Cyril Sargent's "sums" after class.

Chapter 3: Proteus

"Proteus" takes place at about 11:00 A.M. on Sandymount Strand, which is approximately nine miles from Mr. Deasy's school. Stephen wanders along the beach to spend time before he meets Mulligan at The Ship pub at 12:30 P.M. He considers visiting the home of his Aunt Sara and his Uncle Richie Goulding (his mother's relatives), but then he thinks of the ridicule that his father, Simon, has heaped upon Uncle Richie in the past and what Simon might say about today's visit, and he decides not to make the trip. Thus the lengthy description of his visit to the Gouldings concerns only an *imagined* event.

The first two paragraphs of "Proteus" are especially difficult unless one realizes that Joyce, through a stream-of-consciousness technique, is recording the complexity of Stephen's thoughts as he muses upon the question of what is real, and what is not merely appearance. Stephen is a well-read young man, conversant in philosophy as well as in literary theory, and the first two paragraphs mirror his preoccupation with the processes of knowing and being. Although there is probably no exact source that Joyce used for the opening words of the chapter ("Ineluctable modality of the visible"), opening words of the chapter ("Ineluctable modality of the visible"), the subject matter of the following allusions is found in Aristotle's *De Anima*. Aristotle taught that we are first aware of bodies through their translucence or transparency (diaphane), then through their colors. Dante judged Aristotle to be bright and called him *maestro di color che sanno*, "master of those who know."

The first paragraph questions whether what we see is real; the second, the reality of the audible, as Stephen closes his "eyes to hear." The *nacheinander* refers to objects as they are perceived in time – that is, one after another; the *nebeneinander*, as they are perceived in space – that is, one beside the other. The latter deals with visual appearances; the former, with auditory ones. In *Ulysses*, Stephen must disentangle the reality of his past (in Paris as well as in Dublin) from obfuscating memories; he must discover who he really is, as opposed to the person that others, such as Mulligan, perceive him to be.

The parallels in this chapter with Homer are very general. In the *Odyssey*, Menelaus tells Telemachus how he had to deal with Proteus, the god of the sea who could change forms at will. Here, Joyce reveals the changes that are beginning to take place within Stephen, and, through an "interior monologue" technique, Joyce mimes Stephen's shifting thoughts as being like the ever-fluctuating, "protean" nature of reality. The reference to the "winedark" sea pins the chapter to its Greek prototype with its use of a favorite Homeric "epic simile."

Stephen's initial problems in the chapter are philosophical: because all things are bound up in inescapable change ("ineluctable modality"), what is the nature of reality? Does an object exist if no one sees it? Does a sound exist if no creature hears it? Walking along the beach, wearing boots borrowed from Mulligan, Stephen thinks of the many philosophers whom he has read who treated this problem of permanence and change. Aristotle is central among them, as is Bishop George Berkeley (1685-1753), who supposedly denied the objective existence of matter and whom Samuel Johnson purportedly "refuted" by kicking a rock. The capricious nature of reality is epitomized in Stephen's reference to the waves as being the "steeds of Mananaan," the Irish god of the sea, an archetypal jester, who represents change. Once Mananaan resurrected a man from death but put the man's head on backwards, turning his face to the rear – an event which typifies this god of the altered lifestyle.

It is not surprising, then, that in a chapter which concerns the origin and nature of reality, Joyce would insert two women who Stephen pretends are midwives, and these two "midwives" would then make an appearance on the beach, "our mighty mother." These two women are probably from the "liberties," a lower-class section of Dublin, and they are "Florence MacCabe," the widow of Patrick MacCabe, and a lady friend. Mrs. MacCabe carries a heavy bag, and Stephen wonders if it contains a "misbirth." Although this gloomy thought is probably occasioned by Stephen's having been reared in a poor environment, it is soon followed by a variety of witty and humorous associations, as Stephen's emotions rapidly fluctuate. Stephen thinks of certain "mystic monks" whose sashes apparently link them together in the present and trace a path back to God. He envisions all navel cords as extending from Eve, and he wonders whether he could place a call on this "telephone connection" back to "Edenville." His reference to "belly without blemish" is descriptive of Eve, who, as a product of Adam's side, did not have a navel; it also suggests the Immaculate Conception of Mary, the Second Eve, who did not have a mortal blemish in her purity.

The antithesis of this birth imagery is seen in the bloated carcass of the dog sniffed by Tatters and in Stephen's vision of the leprous corpse from the sea. The last, like Milton's Edward King, was sunk beneath the watery floor, but, unlike King, he undergoes no kind of transformation.

Neither does fatherhood escape unscathed in "Proteus," as Stephen wonders who his *real* father is: Simon Dedalus, whose act of love was blind, drunken copulation – or God Himself – Whose "coupler's will" Mary and Simon were simply carrying out, and about Whom there is the command of a *lex eterna* – that is, an eternal law. Stephen, looking towards Dublin's electric power station, the Pigeonhouse, thinks of the blasphemous lines from Léo Taxil's *La Vie de Jésus* (Paris, 1884), in which Joseph asks the pregnant Mary who has put her in this "fichue position," or tough situation; there, Mary answered that it was the pigeon (dove, Holy Ghost, etc.). Thus, Stephen, by implication, shares (symbolically) the nebulous parentage of Christ and of many epic heroes. He is a Telemachus who wonders at this point not *where* his father is, but *who* his true father is.

Stephen's psychological dislocation, then, his ability to see only the "signatures of all things," to hear only their sounds, and not to know their essential selves or *noumena*, leads him to think of his many difficulties, past and present. He remembers the lies that he told about his ancestors at school at Clongowes. He recalls that, while others predicted a fine future for him as a religious man (Stephen was ostensibly a saintly lad), he was really thinking about naked women. He also remembers his ostentatious displays of erudition and his wish to send copies of his early, short prose poems, his epiphanies, to all the major libraries of the world.

The present offers little solace for Stephen. His return from Paris was occasioned by his father's telegram announcing that his mother was dying, and he thinks again of the reason that Buck Mulligan's aunt has forbidden Buck to remain as Stephen's friend: Stephen's refusal to pray at his mother's bedside. He recalls Mulligan's present possession of the key to the Tower. Stephen was afraid of the gypsies' dog, Tatters, and he contrasts himself (again) with Mulligan, who saved a man from drowning. Stephen is supremely sensitive (once again) of his teeth, which he sees as mere shells, an effective image which recalls both Deasy's shell collection in "Nestor" and the beach setting in this chapter. Stephen wonders whether he should use his school pay to see a dentist; then he thinks of the comment made by the anti-Semitic journalist Edouard Adolphe Drumont about Queen Victoria: "Old hag with the yellow teeth."

Stephen's dilemma is defined by Joyce's use of several analogues: (1) Stephen's Uncle Richie sits in bed, calls for whiskey, and "drones bars" from Verdi's *Il Trovatore*; in this opera, the faithful Ferrando is a contrast to the deceiver Mulligan; (2) Jonathan Swift, Stephen feels, was driven mad by the unappreciative rabble and was led to venerate his famous horses in Part IV of *Gulliver's Travels*, the Houyhnhnms; and (3) Kevin Egan, the Fenian whose plans led to disaster; even today, he waits as an exiled "wild goose" in Paris for the resurrection of his native Ireland while trying to enlist assistance for his ideas of revolution.

The original of Kevin Egan, one should note, was Joseph Casey, an Irish Nationalist, who, in 1867, was involved in a tragic attempt to free several Fenians from Clerkenwell Prison in London by using gunpowder. Stephen thinks of Egan (whom he met in Paris) several times in the episode, and Egan fits into several major motifs of *Ulysses*. He is an example of a leader who is abandoned and forgotten by the Irish people. His brand of patriotism, the cause for which he tries to enlist Stephen's help, is a temptation that Stephen must avoid if he is to become a detached, objective artist. In Paris, Egan told Stephen tales of disguise and wild escapes, appropriate to this episode ("Proteus"), which deals with illusion. Finally, Kevin Egan fits into the father theme of *Ulysses*, when he tells Stephen to find Patrice, his son, and let him know that Stephen saw him (Kevin Egan). Patrice is Egan's son by his estranged French wife, and one thinks, in contrast, of the less than febrile passion between Bloom and Molly.

It is no wonder, then, that one of the major analogues for Stephen's plight is the *via crucis*. Two shirts are "crucified" on a clothesline, and in the last paragraph of the episode the spars of the three-master ship, the *Rosevean*, recall Christ's death between two thieves, only one of whom was saved.

Change, to Stephen, is a crucifixion, for he must learn to become mature or be drowned by life, to balance the conflicting forces that define him. As a boy, he was full of dreams and secure, despite belonging to a poor family; he accepted his church's teachings and was scholastically successful, confident of his ability to write fine poetry. Now, after living in Paris, a sojourn which accentuated tendencies towards blasphemy and skepticism which had been present in his personality for a long time, he feels lost. Cut off from the old verities, yet unable to slip into Mulligan's glib, atheistic cynicism, Stephen finds himself defenseless and no longer possessed of a belief in the spontaneity of his genius; he must now walk his deeply troubled Way of the Cross.

Still, however, the chapter is also about hope, and the prognosis for Stephen is not as bleak as some critics have maintained. It is true that there will be no *Tempest*-like "seachange" for the drowned and swollen body, but for Stephen there is at least the strong possibility of renewal; and this rebirth is suggested by two crucial actions. In the first, Stephen, realizing the pretentiousness of his earlier literary endeavors, tears off part of Deasy's letter and begins to write. In the second, he urinates, an action which in much of *Ulysses* is associated with creativity.

With Stephen teetering between solvency—both emotional and monetary—and insolvency, hope and despair, sanity and madness, creativity and waste, the first part of *Ulysses* comes to an end. The capital letter *S* began Stephen's section in "Telemachus"; a capital *M*, for Molly, will begin Bloom's journey in the next section, "Calypso."

The fact that the *S* is used to form part of Mulligan's description ("Stately") and the fact that the *M* is used to form part of "Mr" Bloom's name refer to the interrelatedness of all things. Stephen, even at the start of his own section, needs the gruff masculinity of Buck, and Bloom and Molly heavily (and perhaps ultimately) depend upon one another.

Chapter 4: Calypso

The fourth chapter of *Ulysses* begins at 8:00 A.M. with Leopold Bloom making breakfast in the kitchen of the Blooms' home at 7 Eccles Street. Bloom feeds the cat some milk, walks to Dlugacz's butcher shop to buy a kidney for his breakfast and feels depressed as a cloud covers the sun. He returns home, where he brings in the morning mail (containing a letter from Boylan) to Molly, who is still in bed; he eats his breakfast, then brings Molly's breakfast to her (she is still in bed); Bloom hears church bells and thinks of the funeral for Paddy Dignam, which he must attend. The motif of food in the episode suggests a strong parallel between Bloom of "Calypso" and Stephen of "Telemachus," the two episodes taking place at the same time.

This chapter also parallels the *Odyssey* in that just as Odysseus (Ulysses) was held as a love captive for seven years by the beautiful nymph Calypso, so also is Bloom, in a sense, a prisoner of his wife, Molly. Bloom, however, seems to be a more willing captive than his Greek prototype, and even in his first appearance in the novel, Bloom's bondage is tinged with hints of masochism.

Other evocations of Homer in this chapter include the picture the *Bath of the Nymph,* which Molly has said would like nice hanging over the bed, and Molly's answer to Bloom's definition of metempsychosis as being "the transmigration of souls": "O rocks!" Her retort suggests a mermaid whose shoals mariners (both Greek and Irish) might do well to avoid. In addition, it was believed by some Irish Renaissance popularizers, such as George Sigerson, that Calypso's island, Ogygia, was really Ireland. Although Joyce did not accept this view, he was aware that Gibraltar, Molly's birthplace, was one of the locations that Homer probably used to form his composite of Ogygia.

Bloom is one of the most completely develped characters in all of literature, and in "Calypso," Joyce begins his characterization of his protagonist by sketching many parallels between Stephen (whom we have just met) and Bloom, beginning with the fact that both men leave on their individual odysseys at 8:45 A.M.

Some of the similarities between Bloom and Stephen are not easily detectable at first, but we need to look for them in order to fully understand both men. For example, the first paragraph of this chapter carries through the urinary motif established at the end of "Proteus"; we learn that Bloom's favorite kidneys, mutton ones, contain a "fine tang of faintly scented urine"; Stephen urinated in "long lassoes from the Cock . . . flow[ing] full . . . rising, flowing" in "Proteus." Bloom's cat, with whom he gets along well, reminds one that Stephen has just had a fearful encounter with a dog, and Bloom's cat has a "lithe black form," suggesting the panther that caused Haines's nightmare. In addition, Bloom's visions of the East (containing cattle) resemble Stephen's romantic dreams of the Orient mentioned in "Proteus" and recall Stephen's complicity with Deasy's letter about foot and mouth disease; significantly, Stephen feels that because of his complicity with Deasy, Mulligan will reward him with the title "bullockbefriending bard."

Thus Joyce ties "Calypso" with "Telemachus." Bloom wonders if his cat thinks he is as tall as a tower, and one recalls that Stephen lives in the Martello Tower. Bloom pours the cat some milk that has just been delivered by the milkman, and one recalls the old milkwoman in the opening chapter of the novel. Milly's letter to her father mentions Alec Bannon, and one is reminded of the allusion to Bannon in "Telemachus": "he found a sweet young thing down there. Photo girl he calls her." In an important parallel between Joyce's characterizations of Stephen and Bloom, the cloud which crosses over the sun to depress Bloom momentarily is the same one that affected Stephen's emotions in "Telemachus" and here it is described in almost identical language. In "Telemachus," the cloud triggered Stephen's doleful memory of his mother's death, while in "Calypso," it leads Bloom to think of death: the death of his Jewish heritage, his own aging process, and his desolation of spirit, which makes him cherish the warm flesh of his wife. Bloom's famous depiction of death as the "gray sunken cunt of the world" suggests, with horror, the death of Stephen's mother, Mary Dedalus.

Many of these parallels between Stephen and Bloom that are established in "Calypso" continue throughout *Ulysses*. Both Bloom and Stephen (as was mentioned before) are keyless heroes, both symbolically dispossessed. Bloom realizes that his latchkey is not in his hip pocket, but he does not want to disturb Molly by returning to fetch it from his other pair of trousers. Because Molly has been stirring in her sleep, Bloom simply slips out, leaving the door "to" – that is, closing the hall door just enough to dissuade any possible intruder. Bloom's capitulation to Molly's wishes reminds us of Stephen's deference to Mulligan. In addition, both men wear black – and both men do so because of a death: Mrs. Dedalus's and Paddy Dignam's. As the two men walk through Dublin, at first separately and finally together, they resemble odd Catholic priests: one a Jew and the other an apostate (someone who has forsaken his faith).

In addition, both men are united in their desires to be creative and, for both, writing is associated with bodily functions. Dedalus urinates in "Proteus" after using part of Deasy's letter for beginning a literary endeavor, and Bloom sits in his outhouse reading *Titbits*, and, to wipe himself, he tears off part of the prizewinning story, "Matcham's Masterstroke" by Philip Beaufoy. Beaufoy, in fact, was a real person who did contribute to the magazine, which did, in fact, publish a "prize titbit" in each issue; and Bloom's concern for the money he could make by having a story accepted by *Titbits* ("payment at the rate of one guinea a column") reminds one that Stephen would permit Haines to market his sayings only if *he* were to be paid for their publication. Bloom, the more practical of the two protagonists, seems to be more serious than Stephen in his insistence on commercial considerations. Stephen, in contrast, is being only lightly cynical. Returning to the bodily functions for a parallel, both Stephen and Bloom would agree with Joyce that "dirty [a noun] cleans [a verb]"; here, Joyce's emphasis is on the paradox of the "reconciliation of opposites." In "Proteus," Stephen places a piece of dry mucus on a rock after beginning to write, and here, Bloom contemplates ways of improving his garden through the use of manure mulches.

Besides these similarities in the two men, major differences between Bloom and Stephen also emerge in "Calypso," and they foreshadow the ultimate inability of the two men to be reconciled with one another. Stephen has no home, much less a place to write, but Bloom has, at least, a writing table, albeit it is one that his cat stalks over. Other differences, more profound, concern the inability of the man of science, Bloom, to truly communicate with the with the philosopher-artist, Stephen. Bloom wonders, prosaically, if the cat's tongue is rough so that she can eat more easily; but Stephen wonders if Tatters (in "Proteus") is actually digging up his own grandmother, and he questions whether any so-called reality can be said to truly exist.

Bloom, then, is—in contrast to Stephen, a man of the mind—a man for whom the physical world does emphatically exist, and in "Calypso," Joyce stresses Bloom's acute awareness of the sensations of taste and touch. To say that Bloom eats with relish is no exaggeration, even though the food may be prohibited by Jewish dietary laws. Again, Bloom's solution for a dry mouth is simple: a cup of tea; and while the water for the tea is rising to a boil, there is time to stop by Dlugacz's for a pork kidney.

The shop of Dlugacz, the pork butcher (a Hungarian Jew, like Bloom, and therefore forbidden to eat the food he sells), is a garden of meaty delight for the "peckish"—that is, the hungry protagonist. Having been partially calmed by the aroma of pig's blood, Bloom suddenly becomes apprehensive: the serving girl of the Blooms' next-door neighbors, Mr. and Mrs. Woods, might decide to purchase the last kidney. Bloom finally escapes with his prize, however, and eats it as he reads Milly's letter. He enjoys the repast, and Joyce twice describes him as sopping his bread through the kidney gravy, an ironic contrast to Bloom's behavior in "Lestrygonians" just after 1:00 P.M., when he is forced to leave the Burton restaurant because he cannot stand the spectacle of food being swilled.

Touch is an equally important sense for this sensual man, and Joyce in the chapter frequently depicts Bloom's response to and need for warm objects and people. Bloom quickly notices the bright, pleasant sun, reasoning that it will be a warm day and that he will be uncomfortable in the black suit that he must wear for the funeral. When distressed, he yearns for the warm flesh of Molly, and he imputes the same desire to the cat when, instead of going out of the door as Bloom had thought she might, the animal chooses to go "in soft bounds" up to sleep on Molly's bed, to "curl up in a ball," fetally—perhaps as Bloom might wish to do himself.

Bloom's encounter, from a distance as usual, with the Woods' serving girl in Dlugacz's shop describes a warmth of a different kind: Bloom's sexual awareness, though now lodged in his imagination and physically dormant, will be aroused through Gerty MacDowell in "Nausicaa." In Dlugacz's shop, "blood" becomes the metaphor for sexual life as Bloom's thoughts range from the pig's blood to the tired blood of the Woods couple to the new, vital blood of the maid (and, by extension, to the menstrual blood of Milly and Molly, an important motif in *Ulysses*). Bloom enjoys his slightly voyeuristic memory of the Woods' serving girl whacking a carpet on the clothesline. He apparently likes hefty women, such as his own wife and (possibly) his daughter, and he hopes (but fails) to follow the thick-wristed maid out of Dlugacz's, to walk behind her "moving hams" (another pun on food in this chapter).

In addition, Bloom's trip to the outhouse epitomizes his delight in the physical as he (and Joyce) raise defecation to an art. Although the outhouse episode is probably one of the sections of *Ulysses* that Virginia Woolf found vulgar and disgusting, one must realize that in describing Bloom's modulating his stool, Joyce is offering in reality a bit of praise to humanity and is saying, at the same time, that salvation comes about only through an acceptance of the *total* self. Much of Joyce's work is balanced between scatology (the study of excrement) and eschatology (the study of mankind striving upward towards salvation).

Bloom, then, is portrayed in "Calypso" as accepting and accommodating, the nurturer of life who coordinates the meals and provides sustenance while Molly sleeps. However, this picture of the thirty-eight-year-old Bloom of 1904 is not the only one presented in the novel, and a careful reading of *Ulysses* reveals the tremendous changes that have overtaken the protagonist in recent years. At one time, Bloom was very outspoken—a socialist, a Parnellite, and an ultimate Irish nationalist; he was so outspoken, in fact, that his politics and his personality cost him his employment. And there is a suggestion at the end of *Ulysses* that "Poldy" will regain some of his "spunk"; in fact, Joyce implies in the last chapter, in "Penelope," that Molly will go along with Bloom's demand that *she* bring *him* breakfast in bed.

But in "Calypso," it is the uxorious, or submissive, side of Bloom that emerges. Bloom, for instance, takes pains to prepare Molly's breakfast exactly as she likes it: she insists on four pieces of toast, which must be thin, and the plate must not be full. He acquiesces to her order that he must hurry with the tea. He crawls around, picking up her dirty underwear, to find the risqué book, *Ruby: the Pride of the Ring*, which he finally locates against the orange chamber pot (another instance of creativity being associated with defecation). And he promises to get her another book by Paul de Kock; eventually, he rents *Sweets of Sin*, but neither this book nor *Ruby* is by de Kock: "Nice name he has."

Bloom's streak of fatalism, we realize, may cause a problem for his daughter; he sees in the fifteen-year-old girl the same budding sexuality that Molly possessed at the same age. She fell in love, for the first time, with Lieutenant Harry Mulvey in Gibraltar. Bloom thinks that Milly may lose her virginity to Bannon (she does not); nor did Molly to Mulvey, but he says simply: "Prevent. Useless." On the other hand, Bloom's accommodating, kindly, and permissive nature is revealed in his thoughts of poor Paddy Dignam that end the chapter.

Behind the seemingly clear battle lines of "Calypso," behind the clearly differentiated portraits of Molly and Poldy, a great deal is happening, and Joyce, by cleverly using selective details, suggests the complexities that underlie the surface status quo. This chapter contains many "hidden" activities. For example, Bloom's card bearing the pseudonymous name of Henry Flower is hidden under the hatband of the hat which he bought from John Plasto, the hatter; he will use the card in the next episode to pick up the letter from his pen pal lover, Martha Clifford (undoubtedly a pseudonym, also). In addition, neither Bloom nor Molly wants to acknowledge the letter that she has received from Blazes Boylan; she tries to hide it under the pillow, but its visible torn edge deeply troubles Bloom. On a more humorous level, Bloom slips the kidney from Dlugacz's into a sidepocket, thus hiding it.

Much of the hidden meaning in "Calypso" stems from the upcoming affair between Boylan and Molly. The jingling brass quoits of the bedstead recur throughout *Ulysses*, and they shall be even more ruthlessly tried later in the afternoon. The two lovers will sing "Love's Old Sweet Song" during the upcoming concert tour, but they will practice it at 7 Eccles Street beforehand. It is ironic that Bloom has sent Milly to Mullingar to study photography primarily to get her away from home during his wife's incipient affair with Boylan, since Milly alludes to Blazes in her letter: "Tell him silly Milly sends my best respects."

The implications about the unusual relationship between Molly and Bloom are objectified by Joyce through sexual imagery. *Ruby*, the book that Molly has been reading while sitting on the chamber pot, is about a naked woman who is abused by a sadistic male, suggesting masochistic tendencies in Molly that critics frequently ignore. And one must not forget that Molly likes the *Bath of the Nymph* picture over the bed; the bath, one might note, is taken by naked girls. Bloom, for his part, seems to be defining an aspect of his own nature when he wonders why mice do not squeal when eaten by cats; perhaps, he muses, they *like* it. Many of these ideas will be further developed in Bella Cohen's brothel scene in "Circe."

Chapter 5:   The Lotus-Eaters

This chapter begins at about 10:00 A.M. Bloom has walked approximately a mile from 7 Eccles Street to get to the Westland Row Postal Annex, where he will pick up his letter from Martha Clifford. A careful study of a Dublin street map reveals that Bloom has actually gone out of his way to get to the post office and that, in this chapter, his meanderings form a complete circle. Bloom's circuitous wanderings point both to his guilt over the clandestine correspondence with Martha and to his unwillingness to secure a communication from her that might commit him to take a definite step in their so-far platonic relationship. The wandering also fits in with the dreamy, confused, drugged atmosphere of this chapter, which describes, as it were, various types of "lotus eating."

In Homer's epic, Odysseus and his men come to the land of the lotus-eaters, a hospitable tribe who have a fault: they are generous to excess, offering Odysseus's men a food that makes them forget their quest to return home; some of the crew, of course, eat the flowers and must be physically compelled by Odysseus to leave the country of their soporific hosts. Joyce, as a parallel, saw Ireland as a veritable land of lotus-eaters, its people dwelling in lethargic bondage to the Catholic Church and to their own unrecognized (or unadmitted) sexual yearnings, and he fills this episode with various types of drowsy, sleep-inducing means of escape from reality.

Thus we encounter the slightly dazed Bloom; before he picks up the letter from Martha, he stops before the windows of the Belfast and Oriental Tea Company and reads the "legends" (a pun on the Greek myths) of the tea containers, thinking languourously of the Ceylon blends. He tries to calculate how it is possible that a man can float in the Dead Sea, but his scientific mind deserts him as his reasoning trails off in a series of non sequiturs. Also, when he turns to thoughts of his father's suicide, it occurs to him that he is an "escapist": he did *not* go into the room to look at his father's face, and he is glad that he did not do so. Later, Bloom goes to F. W. Sweny's, the chemist's, in order to pick up some face lotion for Molly; he notices that the shop is filled with lotus land-like items, such as chloroform, and this symbolism is enhanced by Bloom's having forgotten the recipe (prescription) – just as he will forget to return to Sweny's later in the day. In addition, the bar of lemon soap that Bloom takes with him from the chemist's and that will pursue him in "Circe" becomes a symbolic lotus flower, as Bloom sniffs its fragrance. Finally, Bloom ends the chapter by contemplating taking a Turkish bath; he visualizes his penis as a "languid floating flower," or lotus.

Thus much of the activity (or non activity) in "The Lotus-Eaters" records Bloom's desire to escape, to evade the responsibilities of both a wife and a mistress. Bloom doesn't really want an answer from Martha, and, as the postmistress turns to search the postal pigeonhole, he half-wishes that there would be no letter for him: "No answer probably. Went too far last time." He rejects Martha's offer to meet one Sunday after the Rosary and convinces himself that a "love duet" with Martha would be as unpleasant as an argument with Molly; immediately afterwards, he thinks of another lotus image, the narcotic effect of a cigar.

Bloom's wish to escape is a very human trait, and at one point he reveals his deep desire to overcome his loneliness in his city, Dublin, where he feels deeply alienated from his fellow citizens because of his Judaism; he feels that Holy Communion may be a "lollipop" for the faithful, but he reasons that it does permit them to relieve their sense of isolation, to "feel all like one family party. . . . Not so lonely."

Several more allusions to religion in this episode are used to define types of escapism, and they are crucial to an understanding of "The Lotus-Eaters." For example, consider Bloom's thoughts about Martha and Mary and Christ at Bethany. Martha complained because, while she was bustling about the house, Mary simply sat at Christ's feet and listened to His words. Christ reproved not Mary, but Martha, saying that Mary had chosen the better part. The two sisters were the siblings of Lazarus, whom Christ raised from the dead.

The implications of this biblical story for *Ulysses* are manifold: "Martha" is Martha Clifford; "Mary," is Marion (or Molly) Bloom; also foreshadowed here is the fact that Bloom will eventually choose the lethargic Molly (who sleeps with her head at Bloom's feet) instead of choosing the busy typist, Martha. Also, the background story of the good fortune of the resurrected Lazarus contrasts well with the plight of the Dubliners, for whom there seems to be little hope of rebirth or change. Most important, though, is the deliberate setting of the visit by Jesus to the two sisters. This lack of sexual content probably attracted Bloom to the biblical event, and the complex religious symbolism should dissuade any reader from understanding only simple parallels between Christ and Bloom. In "The Lotus-Eaters," Joyce sees Bloom and Christ as being not two martyrs but as being two sexually unfulfilled human beings. Bloom, though, is the sterile one. As he contemplates his bath through Christ's words of consecration over the bread, "This is my body," we realize that, in contrast with Christ, Bloom, at least in "The Lotus-Eaters," is not portrayed as the most "giving" person in the world; Christ, of course, established the Eucharist so that his body could be "given" to all people.

The macrocosm of Bloom's wish to escape from responsibility is epitomized in the microcosm of his inability to enjoy fulfilling sex; and "The Lotus-Eaters" is enhanced by references to all types of jaded sex and to sexual emptiness. Bloom thinks of the *United Irishman*'s charge that the British army in Dublin was infected with syphilis, the association coming after Bloom has just thought of Major Tweedy (Molly's father), that memory, in turn, having been occasioned by Bloom's guilt over Martha's letter. Again, Bloom considers the fanciful notion that Hamlet may have been a woman and that his possible transvestism might have caused Ophelia's death; the reader of *Ulysses* realizes that this time it is Bloom, not Stephen, whose analogue is Hamlet. Also, Bloom is tempted to feel sorry for gelded horses, but he then reasons that they might be happy that way. And eunuchs (having been castrated to be choir boys for the Catholic Church) lead placid lives, even though they do tend to run to fat later in life. Rather parenthetically, Bloom is happy that the two buttons on his waistcoat which were inadvertently left open were not "farther south." Finally, Bloom's contemplated visit to the baths is the culmination of the images suggesting sexual sterility in the chapter. His grand desire is to masturbate (a dead-end type of proposition), and he pictures himself lying in the water with a limp phallus, the very opposite of manly self-sufficiency and masculinity. Languid and limp, Bloom need not make important decisions about sex.

Even when Bloom does contemplate "normal" sex, the result is unfulfilling. Just before picking up his letter, he thinks of the Woods' maid, whom he was *not* able to follow out of Dlugacz's. And his view of the silk stockinged woman in front of the Grosvenor Hotel is blocked by an inopportunely passing tram, as Bloom is reminded of the episode of the preceding Monday when he was denied the sight of a girl adjusting her garter; her companion shielded her from Bloom's view.

Many of Bloom's sexual and other personal problems are illuminated in his preoccupation with the letter from Martha; and in describing Bloom's grossly exaggerated precautions to avoid detection and his desperate eagerness to shake off M'Coy so that he can enjoy the secret missive, Joyce vividly reveals his sense of comic genius.

Martha, for her part, seems to be almost as odd of a duck as Bloom. Her style in the letter is repetitious, trite, and trivial: she feels affronted that the prudent and parsimonious Bloom included stamps with his last letter; she wants a *long* letter from him; and she writes in the language of a Gerty MacDowell – or one of today's *Modern Romance* heroines. Martha is obviously a poor typist as well, leaving off the end of one sentence and committing a grammatical error in subject and verb agreement (one that Bloom remembers in "Hades"): "my patience are exhausted." And in her veiled sexual references, Martha seems to be somewhat of a sadist, as well as a very frustrated Dublin vestal. She twice threatens to punish Bloom, who here seems more like Ruby, the abused circus girl, than like her sadistic trainer; and Martha teases him by her not so subtle suggestion that, since her home life must be unpleasant, she would like to do "something for" him.

Martha's letter fits into the general scheme of *Ulysses* in other ways. She includes with it a yellow flower, suggestive of Bloom's ancestral Hungarian name, Virag (*flower*). Her allusion to her headache implies a menstrual period, "her roses," and thus relates her to Milly and Molly. Her demand that Bloom answer by return mail (with *by return* italicized) ultimately suggests the return of Ulysses-Bloom to his home, and her excuse for calling Bloom "naughty" – that is, the fact that she does not like "that other world" – is properly Joycean in its ambiguity: either Martha does not wish to curse Bloom, or she doesn't wish to risk being sent to that "other world" of Hell or Purgatory for indelicacy; "world" is a misspelling of "word" (as Bloom thinks), perhaps a reference to some profanity that

Bloom included in his last letter to her. Finally, the sentence "Then I will tell you all" beautifully casts Bloom as T. S. Eliot's J. Alfred Prufrock, yet it is unfortunate that no direct influence can be actually proven; for Bloom, like Prufrock, is definitely a man who never forces the moment to its crisis.

In addition to depicting Bloom's sexual misadventures, "The Lotus-Eaters" introduces a number of motifs that will be developed throughout *Ulysses*. One of these is the ad that appears in Bloom's paper, the *Freeman's Journal*, avowing that home is nothing unless it contains a container of Plumtree's Potted Meat. All the words in the short jingle are ironic. To "pot the meat" is slang for sexual intercourse; home is really nothing, even with the product—at least for Bloom, for after Molly and Boylan eat Plumtree's Potted Meat in bed after making love, Bloom later finds some crumbs; and this particular ad looks forward to the Parable of the Plums, which Stephen will recite in "Aeolus" and also in "Ithaca."

Equally important is the "Throwaway" motif, which is introduced when the unsavory Bantam Lyons thinks that Bloom is giving him a tip on the Ascot Gold Cup Race. Later, in "Cyclops," Bloom gets into trouble when the patrons of Barney Kiernan's pub, thinking that Bloom must have won money on the race, wonder why he does not stand them a drink. Actually, Bloom said to Lyons merely that he was going to throw away his copy of the *Freeman's Journal* and that Lyons might as well have it.

The name of the winning horse, Throwaway, has symbolic importance since this twenty-to-one dark horse wins the Gold Cup, besting Sceptre, Boylan's horse. Joyce is suggesting that, although Bloom may at present be "thrown away" by Molly, he may eventually overcome the phallic "sceptre." When Boylan hears that his selection has lost the race—after 8:00 P.M.—he flies into a rage and tears up his tickets in the Blooms' bedroom.

A more humorous motif is started with M'Coy's request that Bloom mark down his name at Dignam's funeral. M'Coy never does show up; yet his name and Stephen Dedalus's name (Stephen does not attend the funeral either) appear in the newspaper, while Bloom's name, though listed among the mourners, is mutilated into "L. Boom." With his request, M'Coy becomes one of the "sinister Dubliners" with whom Bloom has to contend. Fortunately, Bloom was aware of M'Coy's well-known ruse of borrowing valises in order to pawn them, and Bloom is able to escape with his luggage untouched and waiting to be filled for Molly's upcoming concert trip.

Chapter 6: Hades

This episode begins at about 11:00 A.M. outside the house of the deceased Paddy Dignam in Sandymount. Bloom is entering the carriage, which will follow behind Dignam's hearse, together with Martin Cunningham, Mr. Power, and Simon Dedalus (who appears here in person for the first time in the novel). The carriage, which is littered inside with the crumbs of a picnic and, in addition, has mildewed leather, passes an old woman who is peeking at the funeral procession through a window in her house. Bloom spies young Stephen Dedalus, and the other men look at him, Bloom noticing his mourning hat; Simon Dedalus speaks up and curses Buck Mulligan, who he thinks is ruining his son. The carriage also passes Blazes Boylan (just as Bloom is thinking of him), and it also passes a small coffin holding the corpse of a child. The ceremony at the graveside records Bloom's thoughts about death – the contemplations of one who is outside of Catholicism. The chapter ends (still in Glasnevin Cemetery) with Bloom's telling the solicitor, John Henry Menton, of a dent in his (Menton's) hat and being rebuffed for his remark. Menton was defeated by Bloom (by luck) at a game of bowls seventeen years previous (with the young, unmarried Molly looking on), and Menton still holds a grudge.

The conversation of the four men in the funeral carriage relates to several motifs in *Ulysses*. For example, Bloom's memories of his father's suicide, thoughts brought on by Mr. Power's rambling comments, reinforce the father-son theme; and old Rudolph Bloom's dying request that Leopold take care of his dog, Athos (a parallel to Odysseus's faithful old dog Argos), suggests the novel's god-dog concept; the word *Athos*, in fact, contains a hint of the word *theos* – that is, God. Also, the men discuss the son of Reuben J. Dodd, who tried to drown himself because his father insisted that the son end an unsuitable love affair. A boatman saved young Dodd, and his parsimonious father gave him only a florin tip for his troubles; Simon Dedalus's comment, "One and eightpence too much," typifies the personality of this stiff, but often humorous, Micawber-like father. At the graveside, the men see a mysterious thirteenth mourner, a man wearing a Macintosh coat; this is a visitant whose identity will never be disclosed in *Ulysses*, although he will appear in the newspaper report as being one of those at the burial.

Other parallels with the *Odyssey* are very explicit in this episode. Odysseus's anxiety-ridden visit to the Underworld of Greek mythology corresponds to Bloom's trip to Glasnevin Cemetery to bury Dignam, who in turn corresponds to Elpenor, the intemperate follower of Odysseus, who broke his neck in a fall from the roof of Circe's palace. The four rivers of the Greek Hades are paralleled by the four rivers that the men cross on the way to the cemetery: the Dodder, the Liffey, the Grand Canal, and the Royal Canal. As the mourners pass the tenements, they see stripped-up sections of a street, suggesting a means of access to Hades. Among the characters in this section, the kindly Martin Cunningham is a sort of Sisyphus, a Greek symbol of futility: Cunningham spends his life trying to keep out of debts incurred by his drunken wife, who continually pawns the family furniture every Saturday. And Father Coffey, who conducts the funeral service and who is humorously described as a dog, is a sort of Cerberus-figure, who guards the entrance to Hell, or Hades, but who can be compromised by dog biscuits.

In "Hades," Bloom is portrayed as the total outsider, and Bloom's fate, his isolation, is made all the more terrible because, as Joyce goes to great trouble to show, his acquaintances do not intentionally cut him off. He is simply not part of the group. The opening section brilliantly reveals Bloom's separateness: there is no need for the question, "Are we all here now?" since Bloom (who is called by his surname while Mr. Dedalus is called Simon) is the only one left, and needless to say, Bloom enters the carriage last.

Also, it is Bloom that Mr. Dedalus corrects when Bloom tries to look through the paper to find the Dan Dawson speech which has just been mentioned in the carriage (and which will later be quoted and commented upon in "Aeolus"). Dedalus's stilted rebuke reveals a stuffy side of Stephen's father, and it also characterizes Bloom as a blundering anti-hero who can seldom do anything right; but, basically, Dedalus's comment is one that would be made to a social inferior. Again, Bloom suffers when the other three men acknowledge and greet Boylan, the "worst man in Dublin"; Bloom simply cannot understand how three men whom he respects can be attracted to Boylan, and his perplexity leads to even more disquieted isolation.

In addition, Hynes asks Bloom after the burial what his "Christian" name is. Hynes (another decent Dubliner) pays so little attention to Bloom's answer that he garbles his name in a newspaper story, leaving out the "l" from "Bloom," and fails to include "Bloom's" first name at all. Also, the mistake over the name "M'Intosh" comes about because Hynes is only half-listening to Bloom (this incident, interestingly, resembles the mistake over Throwaway in the preceding episode); the mourner is a man *in* a Macintosh coat, not a man called M'Intosh, but Hynes ignores Bloom's "No," his answer to the question, "Is that his name?"

Even when Bloom's friends try to be pleasant, their attempts fail. Mr. Power's questions about Molly's upcoming concert tour suggest Boylan to Bloom, and these questions serve to remind Bloom of the reason why he cannot accompany Molly: he must be in Ennis to commemorate the anniversary of his father's death (June 27, 1886). In addition, Jack Power's inept query about "Madame" doesn't help matters any, but it does evoke the picture for us of Molly as a sort of symbolic whore. Finally, it is sad to see Bloom trying to ingratiate himself with these men who, despite their open and basically good natures, simply do not consider Bloom an intimate.

Nowhere is the gap between Bloom and his three acquaintances greater than in matters of religion. This disparity is perhaps seen best when the men discuss the manner of Dignam's demise. Power thinks that Dignam's sudden death makes him a "poor fellow." Bloom feels, though, that this type of death, like dying in one's sleep, is the best kind. The three men stare at him in wide-eyed silence. To the Roman Catholic, of course, unexpected death is the absolute worst kind of death because the victim has had no time to prepare for it—that is, he has had no time to have confession heard—if he is, by chance, in Mortal Sin. In theory, a drunken, syphilitic Dubliner, dying while asleep, would presumably be dispatched immediately to Hell. But Bloom, possibly influenced by his own father's worn-out end, which culminated in suicide, has no intimation of his conversational faux pas.

In addition, Power's discussion of suicide reveals yet another side of his religious alienation from Bloom: the humaneness of the unbeliever Leopold Bloom as opposed to the cold orthodoxy of Power's brand of Catholicism. Power thinks that suicide is the worst imaginable crime and the greatest disgrace which a family can suffer. For his part, Dedalus believes the act to be cowardly. But the sympathetic Cunningham attempts to soften these strident viewpoints and argues with compassion: even if the suicide did not suffer from temporary insanity, which rules out Mortal Sin (which needs full consent of the will), he says that it is not for us—the living—to judge. Through all of this debate, Bloom, locked in his own world, considers one of the most moving ideas in *Ulysses*: "They used to drive a stake of wood through his [the suicide's] heart in the grave. As if it wasn't broken already."

At times, however, Bloom's divergence from accepted religion, his prosaic, "humanist" contemplation of life and death, leads to a good deal of humor and helps to balance the macabre thoughts of death that Joyce indulges in throughout this episode. To Bloom, the heart is merely a pump, and his matter-of-fact opinion anticipates contemporary medicine. Bloom also cannot accept the Resurrection of the Body, one of the chief tenets of Christianity: "every fellow mousing around for his liver and his lights and the rest of his traps." And Bloom's comment that when the dead Lazarus was ordered by Christ to come forth from the tomb at Bethany, he "came fifth and lost the job," is famous among twentieth-century puns.

In order to contrast the bland but usually good-natured Bloom with the often aloof Stephen, Joyce includes several parallels between "Hades" and "Proteus." Both chapters deal with the beginnings of life and with its end: the old lady on the first page of "Hades" who stares at the carriage, happy that it has passed her by, that it isn't her turn to die yet, reminds one of Florence MacCabe and her friend, mentioned on the first page of "Proteus." At the graveside, the coiled coffinband is referred to as a "navelcord," and one thinks of Stephen's wish to make a telephone call back to Eden, using a telephone wire as a metaphor for all the umbilical cords since the pre-lapsarian Garden. Also, the father-son theme is seen again in Simon's misunderstanding of Stephen: Mr. Dedalus assumes that his son has been at the Gouldings, whereas the reader knows, from "Proteus," that Stephen has decided *not* to visit these in-law "outlaws"; Richie Goulding, whom Mr. Dedalus despises, is the chief of these, and in "Hades" we are told that his back pains are caused by alcohol. Finally, Bloom's judgment that Molly has retained her original, sensual "shape," even though she has put on weight, reminds us of Stephen's musings about appearance, reality, and the shape of objects in the opening paragraphs of "Proteus."

One image pattern more than any other in "Hades" epitomizes Bloom's sad state: the motif of the nails. At the start of the episode, Bloom muses that the nails of corpses are clipped and kept in an envelope (another "dead" letter, like Martha's?). Then later, when the three other men are praising Boylan, Bloom can do nothing but look at his nails. Also, Bloom wonders if Dignam's body would bleed if it were to fall out of the casket and be cut by a nail. Thus the nails have definite Christocentric significance. Bloom is clearly crucified in "Hades," and his death is no more palatable because it comes through the agency of well-meaning friends. He is cut off from the present by the ravine that separates him from the others. His future is most unattractive: Bloomsday, his day, marks the beginning of Molly's affair, and his thoughts return constantly to the past, to the death of his father, Rudolph, and to the death of his son, Rudy.

Chapter 7: Aeolus

The episode begins at noon in the newspaper offices of the *Weekly Freeman and National Press* and the *Freeman's Journal and National Press*. The sprawling building also houses the *Evening Telegraph*, all of the above papers being under common ownership. After the burial of Dignam, the funeral coaches have taken the mourners to the center of Dublin, and Bloom has gone directly to the printing works of the combined newspapers in connection with the advertisement for Alexander Keyes.

The episode corresponds with the *Odyssey* in two main respects. In Homer's epic, Aeolus, the custodian of the winds, gave Odysseus a great boon: all adverse winds, which could hamper his return to Ithaca, were sealed tightly in a leather bag. Within sight of home, Odysseus's men, out of curiosity and greed, opened the bag as their leader dozed, and both the crew and the commander were blown back, off their course. In *Ulysses*, the newspaper headlines, reproduced in large type, parody the often windy, empty journalism that makes up the daily news. And Bloom, within sight of "home" – that is, successfully negotiating the Keyes advertisement – is foiled in his attempt by the demanding Keyes and by the irritation of Bloom's own boss, Myles Crawford, the editor.

Bloom's movement in "Aeolus," form, as it were, a mini-odyssey by themselves, and they must be carefully traced. At the beginning of the episode, it seems that Bloom will have no trouble with the Keyes advertisement. Red Murray cuts out a past version of it and tells Bloom, who is to take the snipped-out square to the *Telegraph* wing of the building, that the *Freeman's Journal* will indeed run a paragraph (gratis), calling attention to Keyes's establishment.

Trouble begins, though, when Bloom meets Councillor Nannetti, the business manager for the *Freeman's Journal*. Nannetti is an Italian and, like Bloom, he is an outsider, but Nannetti has succeeded in making himself accepted by Dubliners and is a member of the Dublin city council. (In fact, the actual Nannetti—Joseph Patrick—served as mayor of Dublin in 1906 and 1907.) Nannetti agrees to print the paragraph about Keyes's establishment, but only with the condition that Keyes guarantees to run the advertisement for three months. Bloom explains that Keyes wants the design of the advertisement changed to a rebus of two crossed keys, a design that appeared in a Kilkenny paper (the *Kilkenny People*) and, furthermore, he will go to the National Library to track down this particular design. This journey will place Bloom in the library at the same time that Stephen is there in "Scylla and Charybdis."

Deciding to call Keyes instead of taking the chance of going to his place only to find that he is out, Bloom enters the office of the *Evening Telegraph* to use the phone. Professor MacHugh, Ned Lambert, and Simon Dedalus are there, and later (but before Bloom leaves for Dillon's Auction Rooms in Bachelor's Walk to find Keyes) J. J. O'Molloy, Myles Crawford, and Lenehan enter the room. Bloom is struck by the opening door when O'Molloy enters, and later he bumps into Lenehan after he finishes his phone call to Keyes; symbolically, there is no room for Bloom in the group. Lambert and Mr. Dedalus leave for a drink at a nearby pub, The Oval, and Bloom leaves to talk to Keyes. As he does so, newsboys mimic his manner of walking, and Lenehan, following their childish lead, does a mazurka to imitate the departing protagonist. After Bloom has left, Stephen and O'Madden Burke enter the office to join Crawford, O'Molloy, Lenehan, and MacHugh.

From this point on, things go downhill for Bloom. He tries to talk to Crawford over the phone but is told (by MacHugh) to come back to the building. (Crawford gives MacHugh the message: tell Bloom to go to hell.) At the exact wrong moment, Bloom, returning, accosts Crawford just as he is leaving the newspaper building; Keyes will accept a renewal, but for only two months, not three. The reply of the irritated and thirsty-for-a-drink editor, that Keyes "can kiss [his] arse," leaves Bloom in a muddle. He simply does not know whether to take Crawford seriously or not. To Crawford, the exchange is a minor contretemps, but, for Bloom, the Keyes advertisement is his major commercial transaction of the day. In effect, Bloom's "return" is as ambiguous as that of Odysseus, who, after a reconciliation with Penelope, had to journey farther, carrying an oar on his shoulder, until he came to a land whose inhabitants had never beheld the sea. Odysseus's bearing an oar blends well with the Christocentric symbolism which surrounds Bloom.

Bloom's frustrated comings and goings here show even more clearly than the events in "Hades" (where the reactions of his fellow Dubliners towards him were muted because of the solemn occasion) his isolation from the people with whom he comes into daily contact. In "Aeolus," for the most part, Bloom is either ignored or treated shabbily. His "third hint" to Hynes about the money (three shillings) that he owes Bloom ("If you want to draw the cashier is just going to lunch") accomplishes nothing. Nannetti's responses to Bloom are curt and terse, even more than the noisy machinery of the printing press necessitates. When Bloom does try to become part of the group by asking what newspaper story is being quoted (Dan Dawson's speech), MacHugh says insultingly that it is a recently discovered fragment of Cicero's; Mr. Dedalus answers in a more kindly manner, perhaps remembering that it was he who diverted Bloom from reading Dan Dawson's speech on the way to Glasnevin. And Lenehan's *Pardon, monsieur,"* when he and Bloom collide is an exaggerated politeness meant to ridicule. Bloom, for his part, as he stands waiting for Nannetti to again acknowledge his presence, seems to realize that he does not have the ability to engage in the light banter, the mild blasphemies that knit Dublin men together; he recalls his rebuff by the pompous Menton (in "Hades") and wishes that he had been able to make a joke about the dinge (dent) in Menton's hat: "I ought to have said something about an old hat or something."

Bloom's plight forms half the episode's "matter"; the conversations of Stephen, Professor MacHugh, O'Madden Burke, Crawford, and the others make up the other half, and the two halves are viscerally connected: the principals in the newspaper office, while dismissing Bloom, worship the lifeless heroes of the past. The great irony of this windy chapter, "Aeolus," is that the true hope of Ireland, Bloom, a man of decency, understanding, and charity, is rejected, while the leaders of Dublin, a professor, a newspaper editor, etc., pursue chimeras.

The conversations in the newspaper office consist of three major topics: the ridicule of the speech which Dan Dawson made the night before; effulgent praise of the mythic reporter Ignatius Gallaher, who "broke" the story of the Phoenix Park murders of 1882 to a New York paper; and the deep respect for a patriotic spech made by John F. Taylor, the orator, in 1901.

The ample quotations from the Dawson speech in "Aeolus," justly parodied by Simon Dedalus and Ned Lambert, show the triteness of Dawson's attitude towards the emerald isle. The speech's many cliched adjectives resemble the descriptive phrases of those who think of Ireland in terms of purling rills and smiling leprechauns. Dawson's speech occludes Ireland's problems as effectively as Haines's shrugging gesture and comment that the land's troubles are the fault of "history." There is irony, though, in the inability of Dedalus and Lambert to see the hackneyed element in themselves, even as they criticize the superficiality of another.

The discussants' bungling of facts about the Phoenix Park murders reveals Joyce's derisive attitude towards those who live in the past. The murders of two high officials whom a segment of the Fenians (the Invincibles) felt were repressing the Irish (they were), took place on May 6, 1882, near the Viceregal Lodge, in Phoenix Park, Dublin. Gallaher, who worked for the *Freeman*, answered the request of the *New York World* for news about the killings by referring the publishers to an advertisement in the *Weekly Freeman* of March 17. By explaining a code in an ad of that day, Gallaher was able to provide details of the assassins' route on May 6. Joyce *may* be implying that the legendary reporter actually knew of the plans for the assassinations before they took place, even though the whole story is, of course, apocryphal.

In any event, Joyce berates the pressmen, including Myles Crawford (who is more drunk than he usually is at noon), by having them place the murders in 1881 instead of the correct year, 1882. It is virtually impossible that Joyce himself slipped in this regar; after all, 1882 was the year of his own birth. Again, Joyce's negative attitude towards Gallaher is defined as early as the short story "A Little Cloud": here, he pictures Gallaher as an apostate Irishman who wears an orange tie, sits enshrouded in a cloud of smoke, and fabricates stories about Parisian sexual excesses.

The John F. Taylor speech was part of the debate over whether the Irish language should be revived. It was impromptu and delivered by a man who had just left a sick bed. So moved is Stephen in "Aeolus," by the quotations from Taylor's discourse, that he is, for the moment, tempted to consider remaining in Ireland to work for its eventual glorification—a seductively deadly trap for an aspiring writer.

The quotations from Taylor synthesize major themes in *Ulysses*: the bondage of Ireland by England is compared to Israel's enslavement by the Egyptians, and those Irish who would urge capitulation to English interests are seen as being no better than the Egyptian high priests who tried to entice the young Moses to give up the cause of freedom. Professor MacHugh, recalling patriots such as Taylor, laments the fact that he must teach Latin, the language of the Roman barbarians, and not Greek (*Ulysses*, when first published as a whole, in 1922, was covered in Greek blue), and he views the British of 1904 as embodiments of the ancient Romans, who were more interested in clean bodies than in pure hearts. The men agree that Ireland needs a Messiah, a Moses, to lead them to a Promised Land, but Moses (like Bloom) was never allowed to enter the land; he received only a so-called *Pisgah Sight* of it, a vision from afar.

Stephen's answer to Taylor's "vision" is his own "vision": his *Pisgah Sight of Palestine or the Parable of the Plums*. His lecture is delivered with only mild sarcasm, for Stephen is portrayed sympathetically in "Aeolus": he is among people who respect him (his father has left by the time Stephen arrives), and he is more at ease than in other episodes, more deferential, and even humble. The meaning of his parable is fairly evident. Two old women (one of whom is probably the same "Florence MacCabe" who appeared in "Proteus") become dizzy as they try to look up at Nelson after they have climbed to the base of his statue. Thus they are caught between two unpleasant alternatives: a stultified Dublin and its imperialistic conqueror. The plum seeds ("stones") that they spit onto the city below through the railings (actually "screenings") are symbols of sterility, in contrast to Boylan's soon-to-be potted meat (Plumtree's). And it is significant in "Aeolus" that a power failure stops the heart of Dublin's life: its trams. Dublins is indeed a paralyzed city.

Finally, "Aeolus," as do all the episodes in *Ulysses*, carries through motifs common to the entire novel. Keyes's demand for two crossed keys at the top of his ad suggests the keyless plight of *Ulysses's* two male protagonists, as does the allusion to "home rule." Bloom's sight of a typesetter reading print backwards reminds him of his father's method of reading his "hagadah book." Lenehan gives the (ultimately incorrect) tip on the Gold Cup: Sceptre. Crawford's act of locking his desk with jingling keys anticipates the jingling bed of Boylan and Molly later that afternoon. Crawford wonders if Deasy was "short taken," when Stephen presents him with the letter about the foot and mouth disease (Stephen tore off part of the letter to write poetry in "Proteus"), and again the theme of creativity and defecation is implied. And, finally, we discover why Deasy is so misogynistic; he has a shrewish wife.

Chapter 8:   The Lestrygonians

This chapter, which begins at about 1:00 P.M. and lasts for approximately an hour, traces Bloom's movements through the center of Dublin. It starts when he observes a Christian Brother buying sweets (presumably for some of his students) and ends when Bloom, evading the approaching Boylan, turns into the National Museum to observe the anal details of the statues of Greek goddesses. In the course of his peregrinations, Bloom is handed a throwaway, a handbill (which recalls for us the racehorse Throwaway), by a melancholy-looking YMCA youth; he feels truly sorry for the ragged Dilly Dedalus (Stephen's sister); he feeds some sea gulls broken fragments of Banbury cakes, which he throws down into the Liffey River; he meets an old flame, Mrs. Breen (formerly Josie Powell); he becomes depressed (again) when a cloud crosses the sun (again); he stops into the restaurant of the Burton Hotel to eat, but is sickened by the piggish manners of the patrons and leaves for Davy Byrne's pub, where he has a glass of burgundy and a cheese sandwich; and, finally, he helps a blind youth cross a street.

In Homer's epic, many of Odysseus's men are devoured by the giant, cannibalistic tribe of Lestrygonians, and this particular episode of the novel is filled with many allusions to eating, a good number of them alluding to disgusting eating practices. The bestial actions of the customers in the Burton restaurant, for example, epitomize the analogy with their Greek prototypes.

The opening pages of "The Lestrygonians" record Bloom's sensitivity towards the passing things of life and remind the reader that Joyce's novel is about the humanity that exists behind the common events of daily existence. A handbill handed to a passing advertising canvasser can, in Joyce's great proletariat novel, relate the canvasser to Jesus; similarly, Bloom, when he hears the first few letters of the YMCA youth's "Blood of the Lamb," thinks that the lad is pronouncing Bloom's name, "Bloo . . . Me? No." Also, other details observed by Bloom, though less obviously "symbolic," are not less human: for example, a sign attached to a rowboat advertising trousers; men wearing scarlet letters on tall white hats, walking around Dublin to call attention to Wisdom Hely, the stationer; and a poor hungry child (Dilly) standing outside Dillon's auction rooms while her father is off drinking. The reader is indeed fortunate that Bloom is such a good observer, for, through Bloom's perceptive eyes, the spectators of today can recreate a Dublin that is long past.

Although he is perceiving physical details with a sharp eye, however, Bloom finds that his thoughts in "The Lestrygonians" constantly return to one subject: the upcoming affair between Boylan and Molly. No matter how often Bloom thinks of the happy times that he has shared with Molly, especially those before the death of their son, Rudy, ten years before (the last time the couple had complete sexual intercourse), the specter of Boylan overshadows his present moments. (Rudy Bloom was born on December 29, 1893, and died on January 9, 1894. Since the death of his son, Bloom has practiced interrupted coitus with Molly, spilling his seed on her rump.) At one point, as he thinks of venereal disease, Bloom's thoughts turn to Blazes: "If he . . . O! . . . He wouldn't surely? . . . Think no more about that." Again, in Davy Byrne's pub, a question by Nosey Flynn causes Bloom to look desperately at the pub clock, which reminds him that it is now two o'clock, just two hours away from the lovers' meeting. Even later, when he thinks of buying a silk petticoat for Molly, the image of Boylan supersedes any possible voluptuousness, even in memory: "Today. Today. Not think." Bloom's thoughts of Boylan seem to bring forth his presence, just as they did when Bloom was on his way to Glasnevin Cemetery; seeing the straw hat and tan shoes that always signal Boylan's appearances in *Ulysses*, Bloom, on the last page of this episode, enters the temporary haven of the museum, clutching his good luck charm, the lemon-scented soap – the *moly* of Odysseus that kept him safe from the enchantress Circe. It is no wonder then that Bloom is forced to compare his wretched present with his past happiness. As he puts it, "Happier then."; Or, "I was happer then." Or, with perhaps the greatest pathos of any single expression in the novel: "Me. And me now."

The first "event" in "The Lestrygonians" is Bloom's meeting with Mrs. Breen, and the details of that chat are crucial to *Ulysses*. Mrs. Breen tells Bloom that her husband, Denis, has gone half mad. His frenzied dream about "the ace of spades walking up the stairs" recalls Haines's nightmare about the black panther, and both images of black prefigure Bloom, who spends the day dressed in mourning clothes. The postcard received by Denis Breen, with the cryptic expression "U.P.: up," has driven him to the offices of Menton the solicitor (returned by now from Dignam's burial in the "Hades" episode) to seek vengeance against the unknown perpetrator; the letters "U.P." *probably* mean "It's all up with you" or "You're dead," although this interpretation is open to question as Joyce includes still another mystery in this novel. Again, Bloom's concern for Mrs. Mina Purefoy ("pure faith"), who has been in labor for three days, indicates Bloom's charitable nature and relates his thoughts to the theme of creativity and birth; yet Bloom confuses the beleaguered mother's name with that of Philip Beaufoy, author of "Matcham's Masterstroke"; Bloom, one might recall, "tore away half [of this] story" in "Calypso" to wipe himself. Finally, the appearance of Lamppost Farrell, an actual Dublin eccentric who dressed like a madman and superstitiously always walked on the outside of lampposts, is coupled with the incipient madness of Denis Breen to paint a most untowardly (though comic) picture of Dublin society. More important, though, is the dreadful toll that the madness of life has taken upon Mrs. Breen, and Bloom marvels that this ravaged woman is only a year or so older than Molly. Thus Mrs. Breen, as well as Bloom, fits the sad theme of "Me. And me now."

Leaving Mrs. Breen and then passing the offices of the *Irish Times*, Bloom recalls the ad that led him to Martha Clifford, and the reader is able to fill in important background information. Bloom thinks that there may well be other responses to his advertisement awaiting him at the *Irish Times*, in addition to the forty-four answers that he has already gone through, but he decides to "leave them there to simmer."

The original ad read, "Wanted smart lady typist to aid gentleman in literary work," and Bloom thinks of one respondent, Lizzie Twigg (an actual poetess), who had been praised by "the eminent poet A.E.," George Russell, the theosophist, as well as poet, who will figure prominently in the next episode. The "conservative" Bloom, however, thought that Ms. Twigg might be too bohemian or arty. A little later in the chapter, Bloom sees Russell bicycling by, accompanied by a young woman who might be Lizzie Twigg: "Coming events [witness the appearances of Boylan] cast their shadows before."

Unable to eat at the Burton Hotel because of the disgusting spectacle of its wolfing, slobbering customers, Bloom enters the pub of Davy Byrne, a "moral pub," and the reader finds out a good deal more about the protagonist's character. Buoyed up temporarily by a glass of burgundy and a cheese sandwich, Bloom thinks of the moment in the spring or summer of 1888 when Molly agreed to marry him, on the hill of Howth, overlooking Dublin Bay. In this deeply romantic reminiscence, parts of which will recur several times in *Ulysses*, we discover a side of Bloom that has not yet been revealed, one that makes Molly's upcoming sexual union with the insensitive Boylan—which the emotionally exhausted Bloom is unable to prevent—all the more important to our understanding of Bloom. Although the description of Molly's passing the warm and chewed seedcake (of life) from her mouth to Bloom's has often been glibly subjected to Freudian analysis by literary critics, the picture presented of Bloom in this "Garden of Eden" is not primarily that of a son being "fed" by a mother, but of a vital, passionate lover, able to inspire the same emotion in another human being. We must not forget (Bloom certainly does not) that while the sensual Molly had many suitors, Bloom is the man whom she did, in fact, marry. Had he not spent that beautiful moment under the wild ferns on Howth with Molly, Bloom might, at times, border on the farcical. The deep love that Molly held for him, at least sixteen years ago (and perhaps now), adds necessary depth to Bloom's portrait.

Still another positive side of Bloom is revealed in the conversation between Nosey Flynn (who appeared first in Joyce's short story "Counterparts" in *Dubliners*, and who received his nickname from his habit of always "snuffling it up") and Davy Byrne, after Bloom has left for the bathroom. Flynn says that Bloom is a Freemason (and therefore immediately set apart from Dublin Catholics), "in the craft." Yet Bloom is a good man, and the two men praise his temperance ("God Almighty couldn't make him drunk") and his charitable nature ("He has been known to put his hand down too to help a fellow"). The latter praise is especially important, for it foreshadows Bloom's helping the fallen Stephen in "Circe," after the young man has been struck by Private Carr and knocked to the ground. In general, then, Byrne and Flynn think a good deal of Bloom ("Decent quiet man he is"), even though Bloom is reluctant to, as they put it, "put anything in black and white" – that is, make a contract or an agreement. However, even in this temporary place of refuge, Bloom is misunderstood, and after Bloom has left, Bantam Lyons once again spreads the lie that Bloom has given him a tip on the Gold Cup race.

Chapter 9: Scylla and Charybdis

This episode takes place in Dublin's National Library from 2:00 P.M. to 3:00 P.M. In this intricate chapter, Stephen further explicates his theory about Shakespeare and *Hamlet* that Mulligan asked him to explain to Haines in "Telemachus." Stephen's brilliant but difficult exposition is made even more perplexing by the fact that he himself does not truly believe all of his own theories about Shakespeare – or even about Hamlet; in his own words, his arguments to the men in the library are a "performance." Thus, while the chapter does not tell us a great deal about Shakespeare's personal life (despite the many interesting points about the playwright that it does raise), it tells us very much about Stephen himself, particularly his obsession with paternity; this episode explicitly deals with the father-son theme of the novel: at the conclusion of the chapter, for example, Bloom walks between Stephen and Mulligan as the two young men are about to walk down the library steps; he forces them, symbolically, to separate. This act, besides foreshadowing other sunderings in *Ulysses*, links the older Bloom with youth, and with Stephen in particular.

In Homer's epic, Odysseus was forced to pass between the six-headed monster, Scylla, and the whirlpool, Charybdis. Following the advice of Athena, he hugged the mountain lair of Scylla; Charybdis, he had been told, promised certain disaster, and he sacrificed one of his men for each of Scylla's maws. In *Ulysses*, the whirlpool is represented mainly by the poet A. E. (George Russell), an exponent of mysticism, Platonism, and emotive Irish nationalism. Stephen is, as it were, Scylla, constantly snapping at the arguments of his opponents; he is possessed of a sharp, cutting, Aristotelian mind and is, as Mulligan called him earlier in jest, Kinch, the knifeblade.

Joyce adds complexity to the Homeric parallel by comparing Stephen to Scylla, an "enemy" of Odysseus-Ulysses (Bloom). In a sense, Stephen, with his carping logic, *is* an opponent of the more mundane and practical Bloom, and, in the later stages of *Ulysses*, Joyce portrays the impossibility of the two men's reaching any satisfying or permanent relationship. Also, by placing Stephen in a generally Homeric context, Joyce suggests that Stephen must go through his own odyssey in the novel – that is, he must attempt to reconcile the flesh with the spirit, the mind with the body, and his "deep" and grandiose thoughts with workaday concerns. Finally, it may well be plausible to see the six-headed hydra, Scylla, in the six principals with whom Stephen debates: Lyster, Best, Russell, Eglinton, Mulligan, and Stephen himself in his role as a self-doubting skeptic who does not believe his own theory of Shakespeare or any other "theories," including religious teachings, that he has come across thus far in his life.

The episode opens with Stephen disputing aesthetics, the new Irish writers, and other matters with the Quaker librarian, Thomas William Lyster, Director of the National Library; with John Eglinton, an influential Anglo-Irish essayist and editor of the short-lived journal *Dana*; and with Russell. They are soon joined by Richard I. Best, Assistant Director of the National Library. Russell's leavetaking ends the initial section of "Scylla and Charybdis."

Stephen begins to deliver his Shakespeare thesis, but other thoughts intrude upon his consciousness. He notices, for example, that John Eglinton trumps Stephen's theories with an "elder's gall"; and, to counter Eglinton, Stephen forces himself to smile in the manner of his former confidant Cranly, who figured prominently in Book Five of *A Portrait*. He then remembers the telegram that he sent to Mulligan at The Ship pub, canceling their luncheon appointment. A mention of Haines causes Stephen to feel guilty: he has smoked Haines's tobacco and, in general, he has treated the Englishman badly. Stephen also remembers the money that Russell lent him for food (which Stephen spent on a prostitute, Georgina Johnson), and he is reminded of Deasy's injunction in "Nestor" that a man's proudest boast should be that, despite all, he "paid his way"; thus when Stephen muses upon his indebtedness to Russell, it gives rise to the notorious pun "A.E.I.O.U.," after he has thought of another "father figure," Father Conmee, S.J., who saved Stephen from a whipping when he was a boy at Clongowes Wood College (actually an elementary school) in Book One of *A Portrait*. In this general context of guilt, Stephen is also reminded of his mother's death, and we learn that despite his somewhat priggish refusal to pray at her bedside, he did indeed weep for her: "I wept alone." As Stephen speaks of Anne Hathaway's seduction of young William Shakespeare, a woman several years Shakespeare's senior, Stephen cannot help but muse about his own future and wonder when some buxom wench, some "greyeyed goddess," will "overtip" him in a cornfield: "And my turn? When?"

The pathos of Stephen's situation is clearly portrayed in the callous conversation that attends Russell's leavetaking to return to the office of *The Irish Homestead*, the farmers' periodical (the "pigs' paper," according to Stephen), that A.E. edits. The principals discuss a gathering of the Dublin literary intelligensia to be held that evening at the residence of the novelist George Moore. Stephen has not been invited to it, although Mulligan has been and, in fact, Mulligan has been asked by Moore to bring Haines with him. Also, the men discuss a "sheaf of our younger poets' verses" that Russell is editing. Significantly, Stephen has not been asked to contribute to the collection. The sheaf, in actuality, was a fifty-six-page compendium of poetry from such rising Irish Renaissance figures as Padraic Colum and Seumas O'Sullivan and appeared under the title *New Songs* in 1904. Padraic Colum's thirty-six-line poem "The Drover" is singled out by the discussants at the library; they hope that *The Daily Express* (for which Gabriel Conroy writes reviews in Joyce's short story "The Dead") will give the volume a boost.

Using all of this chatter, Joyce intends to demonstrate that Stephen is not considered an equal by the other men; he is as much of an outsider among his fellows as Bloom is among his. Thus, another point of similarity between the two men emerges: with neither Bloom nor Stephen are the protagonists' friends actively hostile; they simply do not feel that Bloom and Stephen are their equals. Russell, in a kindly but certainly patronizing way, promises to publish Deasy's letter, but only after reminding Stephen that "we have so much correspondence."

Again, the exchange surrounding Russell's parting demonstrates Joyce's brilliant alteration of background data to shape an artistic end. *New Songs* appeared in April of 1904, and Joyce changes the date to portray the publication as an impending one; and Stephen is excluded from *New Songs* (as was Joyce). Also, although Stephen testily derides Russell's magazine, Joyce did publish three short stories in *The Irish Homestead* in 1904.

In the first part of "Scylla and Charybdis," then, Stephen is definitely not a part of the Irish Literary Renaissance, a movement that Gaelic proponents hoped would restore Ireland's national image. His views are quite different from those of Douglas Hyde, who, in his *Love Songs of Connacht*, 1893, found inspiration in the untutored passions and language of the country people of western Ireland. Nor does Stephen overly admire John Millington Synge, even though his play *In the Shadow of the Glen*, 1903, provoked a great deal of discussion in Ireland because of its portrayal of a loveless Irish marriage, with the wife leaving her husband to follow a tinker.

Given the disparity between Stephen and his interlocutors, it is no wonder that his theories about the enigmatic Shakespeare seem a bit arcane. They certainly differ from Lyster's, as the reader discovers at the opening of the chapter. Lyster, the Quaker librarian, who cites Goethe's *Wilhelm Meister's Apprenticeship*, 1796, believes, as did Goethe, that Hamlet's problems stem from ineptitude in his character, from his being an "ineffectual dreamer." Goethe, as the English poet Coleridge was to do some two decades later, believed Hamlet to be a sensitive prince who was too immersed in the subtleties of his own personality to act in a "manly" way. (Of course, both Goethe and Coleridge ignore the fact that during the play, Hamlet does manage to kill several people.) Russell, who constantly stresses the idea that modern exegetes have no right to peer into the biographical data of the Bard, finally appears naive, when compared to the complex Stephen. To Russell, it matters not whether Hamlet is Shakespeare's fictional portrait of Essex or James I. To him, only the "formless spiritual essences" are important, and he objects to "prying into the family life of a great man." But if the portrait of Russell can be explained as mere caricature by Joyce, who felt that the Irish Renaissance was a wasteful illusion, certainly the citation of the French poet Mallarmé, sentimentally believing that Hamlet was walking about "reading the book of himself," cannot be so easily dismissed; he alludes to a town poster announcing a performance of *Hamlet* with the subtitle "Le Distrait," the absent-minded or distracted one.

Stephen, obsessed with the ghosts of his own past, including his mother (a parallel with *The Odyssey* in which Odysseus met his own mother in Hades), believes that Shakespeare himself was very much like King Hamlet of Denmark, who appears as a ghost to his son. And to begin his thesis, Stephen pictures the Globe Theater as it was in Shakespeare's day: "The play begins." Stephen's method is "composition of place," a technique which the founder of the Jesuits, St. Ignatius Loyola, used in his *Spiritual Exercises* to help believers summon up a physical picture of the locale of a spiritual mystery. For example, the novice tried to imagine the dress that Mary was wearing when Gabriel appeared to her to announce that even though she was still a virgin, she would be the mother of God, and, in addition, the novice was expected to picture what the angel looked like. Joyce employed this method of artistic detail to describe Hell in Book Three of *A Portrait*, and Stephen uses the same technique in "Scylla and Charybdis."

In Stephen's scheme of things, then, Shakespeare himself, prepared by a professional acting career, played the part of the ghost during the first performance of his masterpiece. Moreover, Hamnet Shakespeare, the Bard's son, had he lived, would have been the same age as the protagonist. And Hamnet-Hamlet's part is played by the great tragic actor Richard Burbage, spoken to by Shakespeare himself; thus, symbolically, Shakespeare spoke to his "son" about the sexual infidelities of Anne Hathaway Shakespeare (Gertrude).

Perhaps the most important parts of Stephen's theories are his conclusions that he outlines before the appearance of Buck Mulligan and which he develops in detail while Mulligan derogates Stephen's assumptions. One of these conclusions is that Shakespeare never recovered from the emotional wound inflicted by Anne Hathaway, who seduced him, and Stephen insists, later cuckolded him. Thus, before it became fashionable to do so, Joyce maintains (through Stephen) that *Hamlet* is a psychosexual drama: King Hamlet, first of all, is a betrayed husband and only afterwards a murdered monarch. Because of his father's death, Hamlet the Prince becomes "dispossessed," his loss of a home and kingdom matching the losses of Stephen and Bloom, the two keyless heroes whose positions have been usurped. (Of course, Gertrude as betrayer becomes an analogue for Molly Bloom.) A second conclusion drawn in the opening rounds of the *Hamlet* debate comes from Stephen's brilliant turning around of the adage that Shakespeare's last plays are about reconciliation: Stephen argues that in order for there to be a reconciliation, there has to have been a sundering, and it is the sunderings in Shakespeare's life – among his family and friends – that Stephen considers, after he recovers from the surprise of Mulligan's entrance into the library.

But the appearances of Mulligan – and of Bloom – do provide much needed comic relief from the intricacies of Stephen's exposition, while the long pages of exposition continue Joyce's major themes. The grand entrance of Buck Mulligan follows Stephen's summary statement about *Hamlet*, that the "son [is] consubstantial with the father" – that is, Shakespeare is both King Hamlet and Prince Hamlet, and by implication, that Joyce is both Stephen and Bloom in *Ulysses*. (Stephen is the age of Joyce in 1904 – twenty-two; and Bloom, the age of Joyce – thirty-eight – when the major sections of *Ulysses* were being composed.) The term *entr'acte* refers to a break between the acts, and Mulligan's blasphemous humor (seen before in "Telemachus") resembles the combination of piety and broad farce found in medieval "interludes" and also in the gravediggers' scene in *Hamlet*.

Mulligan's scorn falls on all alike: on Shakespeare ("I seem to know the name"); on Synge, because of Yeats's elaborate comparison of him to Aeschylus; on Stephen, because of his mystio-biographical interpretation of all reality ("The aunt is going to call on your unsubstantial father," a parody of Stephen's musings about consubstantial fatherhood, which Mulligan overheard as he was entering the discussion room); and even on Bloom – especially on Bloom, who, Mulligan detects, is Jewish. Poor Bloom, the eternal loser, the Irish Charlie Chaplin, has failed once again. In spite of all his elaborate precautions, he has been *observed*, staring at the anus of a museum goddess! And of all the people in Dublin to discover him, it was Buck Mulligan. Looking at Bloom's name on the card that he fills out to examine the *Kilkenny People* file (for the Keyes ad), Mulligan ties together several strands in *Ulysses* as he turns suddenly to Stephen and says, "He knows you. He knows your old fellow [Simon, Stephen's father, a brief reference to the father-son theme]. O, I fear me, he is Greeker than the Greeks [a pederast, but also a reference to the Greek Odysseus]. His pale Galilean eyes [Bloom paralleled with Christ] were upon her mesial groove."

Yet Mulligan, to give him his due, reveals his admirable buoyancy when he praises Stephen's wit in the telegram that informed Mulligan that Stephen would not meet him for lunch. Although Mulligan calls the telegram a "papal bull," emanating from the lapsed

Jesuit Stephen, Mulligan thinks that sending it was "wonderful inspiration!" The telegram's quotation about the sentimentalist is a paraphrase of a passage from George Meredith's *Ordeal of Richard Feverel* (1859); it probably refers both to Mulligan's blithe habit of literary borrowing and to his refusal to look seriously at traditions which he ridicules.

Just before the allusion to Meredith and the telegram, however, a much more important passage occurs, one in which Mulligan, significantly does not take part. This concerns the discussion of Oscar Wilde's *Portrait of Mr. W. H.* (1889), which argues that "Mr. W. H.," the person who Shakespeare said was the inspiration behind his sonnets, was really a boy actor named Willie Hughes. Of course, references to the mysteries behind the sonnets were not new to Joyce, and naturally the discussion does add to the mystifying "Charybdis" tone of the entire episode, but one wonders why Mulligan does not say anything when the theory of the homosexual Wilde is brought up. Mulligan, after all, is the one who humorously suggests that Stephen should be wary of Bloom's sexual preference; this possible homosexuality of Mulligan has tantalized many critics.

Continuing his theory about Shakespeare after the Mulligan *entr'acte* has ended, Stephen goes on to examine the character of Anne, who was, he feels, scarcely a faithful Penelope who remained in Stratford awaiting the return of her long-absent husband. Dismissing Shakespeare's rumored pederasty and his affairs with London slatterns as symptoms more than causes, Stephen maintains that the great wound of the Bard's life came *after* his marriage—when Anne betrayed him. His proof of this point, which was implied earlier in the episode, is twofold: Shakespeare never mentions Anne in all thirty-four years of his marriage to her, and he left her only his second-best bed as a legacy, after excluding her entirely from his first will. Stephen counters the tired arguments that center around the "second-best bed" by chanting in blank verse to the somewhat "blank" John Eglinton and by pointing out that such a bequest would have been an insult to the survivor, coming as it did from such a wealthy playwright, as Shakespeare would (or should) have been.

Nor does Shakespeare himself escape unscathed from Stephen's critical examination. Stephen feels that in many ways Shakespeare was extremely narrow minded. He was parsimonious, and to some extent Shylock and Iago are self-portraits. He capitalized upon popular (and "conservative") causes: anti-Semitism and voyages of discovery to the New World, such as the one to Bermuda that is believed to have inspired *The Tempest*. Also, Shakespeare transmogrified into art certain hostilities that he felt towards his two "usurping" brothers, Richard and Edmund; the mesomorphic Gilbert doesn't count: "The playhouse sausage filled . . . [his] soul."

Richard Shakespeare, according to Stephen, became in Shakespeare's works the unredeemed villain Richard III, and Edmund became the illegitimate, literally usurping son of Gloucester in *King Lear*. Stephen draws great significance from the fact that the last four acts of *Richard III* seem simply grafted on to the courtship of the ugly Richard and Lady Anne in Act I, and the autobiographical reference to Shakespeare is obvious. In *King Lear*, Stephen maintains, the Edmund subplot really has no relevance to the ancient Celtic myth.

Stephen's view of Shakespeare, then, encompasses many aspects of the human psyche and indeed the soul: the Procession of the members of the Holy Trinity; the relation of the past to the present; the nature of change, which always returns upon itself ("We walk through ourselves. . . ."); and the permanence of love. Basically, however, Stephen's exposition is an elaborate effort to try to identify his own place in life. His mother is dead; his father, though well meaning at times, is separated from him by an abyss of temperament. And, so far, Stephen has not succeeded in living up to the mystical and metaphorical components of his name ("What's in a name?"); he has tried to leave Ireland, to fly from its entanglements like the "hawklike man," Daedalus, but he has been forced to return to earth. He is more like Icarus, whose wings melted when he flew too close to the sun.

After Stephen's intellectual acrobatics, "Scylla and Charybdis" returns to more mundane matters. Stephen is criticized by Eglinton for demanding money for the publication of his ideas in *Dana*; another reference is made to Moore's upcoming get-together; Lamppost Farrell is sitting in the library's readers' room; Mulligan chides Stephen for his derogatory review of Lady Gregory's *Poets and Dreamers* in *The Daily Express* (March 26, 1903); and Mulligan recites his hymn to masturbation, "Everyman His own Wife." It is this last episode that finally convinces Stephen that there are "seas between" him and Mulligan, and coinciding with this distressing insight is Stephen's perception that there is someone behind him, the someone being Bloom, who is also leaving the library.

This linking of events strengthens the importance of the last several lines of this chapter. Stephen remembers that he once stood upon the library steps and interpreted a flock of birds as being an augury of his own destiny (Chapter Five of *A Portrait*), and the reader wonders if the symbolically rich sundering of Stephen and Mulligan—necessitated by Bloom's passing between them—will augur well for the young protagonist. Stephen's dream of the exotic East and the "creamfruit melon" foreshadows Bloom's kissing his wife's melons (buttocks) in "Ithaca." The allusion to Bloom as the Ancient Mariner places Stephen in the position of the Wedding Guest, one able to learn from the more experienced canvasser. And Mulligan's warning to Stephen to beware of Bloom ("Get thee a breechpad") is much more indicative of Mulligan's own latent homosexuality than of any nefarious intent on Bloom's part. In fact, with the charity that the Dublin Jew lends to Stephen, Bloom emerges in the novel's later chapters as the young man's true "father," the mystical father who, Stephen believes, is related to the son in "a mystical estate"—in contrast to physical paternity, which may be, according to Stephen, "legal fiction."

Chapter 10: The Wandering Rocks

This episode begins at 2:55 P.M. and ends at 4:00 P.M. It describes the wanderings of several characters from *Ulysses* around the streets of Dublin, and thus it forms a mini-odyssey, a microcosm of Joyce's novel. The chapter consists of nineteen short episodes which mirror the overall eighteen-part structure of Ulysses (early critics usually described "The Wandering Rocks" as consisting of eighteen parts and a final *coda*, the description of the viceregal cavalcade). Coming as it does after the first nine sections of *Ulysses* (traditionally accepted to be the first "half" of the novel), "The Wandering Rocks" is a kind of interlude—much like the comic entrance of Buck Mulligan during Stephen Dedalus's discussion of Shakespeare in "Scylla and Charybdis"—before Joyce begins the second "half" of the novel.

The chapter is almost perfectly balanced: the meanderings of Father Conmee, S. J., the amiable, patronizing former rector of Clongowes (who once saved Stephen from a painful punishment in *A Portrait*) begin the episode, and the cavalcade of the amiable, patronizing William Humble Ward, Second Earl of Dudley as he travels to open the Mirus Bazaar ends the chapter. The two men represent Ireland's bondage to two key foreign powers – the Roman Catholic Church and Britain – and all of the smaller odysseys in the episode are directly related to these two major structuring devices. Also, it is in the middle section (the tenth section) of "The Wandering Rocks" that Bloom rents *Sweets of Sin* for Molly. Finally, this near-central chapter of *Ulysses* is tied together by scores of motifs, gestures, thoughts, and cross-references. Joyce apparently wrote "The Wandering Rocks" with a map of Dublin before him, and modern Joyceans take great delight in *timing* the various wanderings of the participants, one critic going so far as to limp along the Dublin streets, miming the one-legged sailor; he discovered that Joyce was unusually accurate in his time sequences.

Parallels with Homer's *Odyssey* are especially clear in this chapter. In Homer, Circe told Odysseus that to return home he must sail either through the large, moving ("wandering") rocks or else he must pass between Scylla and Charybdis. Because only the mythological Jason of the Argonauts had succeeded in negotiating the rocks, Odysseus chose to battle Charybdis, the whirlpool, and Scylla, the six-headed monster.

Joyce, however, is having fun at the reader's expense in this chapter because, to read *Ulysses*, the reader must pass through *both* the treacherous rocks *and* the labyrinth of the National Library, with Stephen's complex intellectual expositions at its center. Also, in Homer, the wandering rocks were probably based on optical illusions, and Joyce has correspondingly filled his rendition of the myth with "false clues" and deliberately misleading language. He seems to be saying to the reader: "You've come through nine episodes, and you think that you really know Dublin – and my writing methods. Beware: you are being over-confident; Dublin and my writing methods are neither simple nor easily grasped."

These tricks of Joyce, escorting us by circuitous ways through the various routes in and around Dublin, begin at once. Father Conmee, we are told, "reset his smooth watch"; he did not, however, correct the time. Instead, he "reset" it – that is, he placed it in his pocket. In addition, we are told twice that Father Conmee is walking through Clongowes' playing fields; this is not literally true: he is returning to his old school ground in Clongowes in his *memory*. Also, note that Blazes Boylan's secretary, Miss Dunne, wonders whether "he [is] in love with that one, Marion," while she is thinking of William Wilkie

Collins' *Woman in White* (remember, Boylan is readying himself for a rendezvous with Marion Bloom); "that one," however, here, is really Marian Halcombe, a *woman* character in Collins' novel. Moreover, Bloom does not buy *Sweets of Sin*; rather, he rents it, as we discover in "Ithaca." In addition, Father Cowley is not a priest in good official standing with the Church; he is a "spoiled priest," simply "Bob" Cowley, a fellow in financial straits. Bloom the dentist has no connection with the protagonist; Denis Breen never does see the solicitor John Henry Menton, but leaves his office after an hour's wait, and later makes a faux pas when he salutes the carriage carrying Gerald Ward instead of the carriage of the Earl of Dudley; and Lamppost Farrell, who bumps into the blind stripling (the youngster whom Bloom helped in "The Lestrygonians"), is figuratively "blinder" than the lad. In all this ambiguity, however, one thing is certain: Mulligan's statement made to Haines as they both sit drinking tea certainly proves to be prophetic: "He [Stephen/Joyce] is going to write something [*A Portrait*] in ten years."

If employment of deceit or ambiguity is a *modus operandi* in this episode, ironic contrast of "factual" events is another. Joyce uses his recurrent images and happenings to express a sardonic theme, and his motifs are very skillfully employed. Father Conmee's holy thoughts are juxtaposed against the sudden appearance of the flushed young lover and the young woman who cross his path (and who later turn up in "The Oxen of the Sun"). The arc of Corny Kelleher's "silent jet of hayjuice" is matched against the "plump bare generous arm" of Molly Bloom, as she throws a coin in an arc to the crippled sailor in the third episode of this chapter. Lenehan's comment that Bantam Lyons is giving out tips on the hopeless darkhorse Throwaway, false information which he originally received in the mixup with Bloom in "The Lotus-Eaters," is quickly followed by the appearance of Bloom himself looking for a sexy novel to bring home to his wife ("A darkbacked figure scanned books on the hawker's cart") and by a "skiff," the Elijah, "a crumpled throwaway," which floats (voyages) down the Liffey River throughout the episode. And the snippet from the patriotic, anti-British song "The Croppy Boy" ("*At the siege of Ross did my father fall*") is juxtaposed against Mr. Kernan's subservient rush to see the viceregal cavalcade.

Joyce's use of contrast is most effective in the fifth section of "The Wandering Rocks." Here, Boylan tells the girl from Thornton's to put a bottle of wine (meant to warm up Molly before his visit) in the bottom of the bag of fruit and to deliver it at once to "an invalid." Not content with the upcoming visit, however, he flirts with the clerk; he looks down into her blouse, and Joyce records for the reader the *only* unspoken thoughts of Boylan that we are told of in the whole of Ulysses: "A young pullet." Yet while the aggressive, sexually indefatigible Boylan contrasts with the sensitive, passive Bloom (who is getting his sexual pleasure vicariously in this section by glancing through pornography), it is Bloom, the "throwaway," who may at last triumph. Joyce makes it clear that Boylan is a mere stud: he reduces everything to sex, and to him women are less than human.

In "The Wandering Rocks," Joyce uses his "false clues" and his ironic contrasts or juxtapositionings to express a human theme, and his art becomes a means of creating a grand Chaucerian pilgrimage. As do many great artists, Joyce accepts people largely as they are, and "The Wandering Rocks" forms his panorama of Dublin's city dwellers with all their warts. The point of view in "The Wandering Rocks" is naturalism tinged with compassion. For example, though Father Conmee may be a bit condescending, he does truly care for people, in particular about those outside of the Catholic faith who may die in "invincible ignorance" and never gain heaven; he may like "cheerful decorum," but he is nonetheless concerned about the plight of the "African mission" and about the dark souls of natives who will never receive "baptism of water. . . ." And Father Conmee can only bless the one-legged sailor because, by the rules of his order, he has taken a vow of poverty; he does not have money to spare for the beggar. As another example of Joyce's attitude toward Dubliners, note that in the ninth section, M'Coy's "putdown" of Lenehan is deftly carried out and, because of its understatement, it realistically portrays the reactions of a jokester who fails and his slightly stiff listener. Lenehan tells of taking liberties with Molly (with her "milky way") during an evening in 1894 while Bloom was pointing out the constellations of the stars as the group of old friends returned from the "big spread out at Glencree reformatory. . . ." Taken aback by M'Coy's cool response to his off-color anecdote, Lenehan is forced to admit about Bloom: "He's a cultured allroundman, Bloom is. . . . There's a touch of the artist about old Bloom."

Joyce's compassion for the Dubliners in "The Wandering Rocks" is perhaps most evident in his family portraits, and it is unfortunate that some critics tend to overemphasize the humorous side of the episode; in it, Joyce incorporated several unforgettably moving scenes. Just a few of these include (1) Maggy Dedalus's telling her hungry sisters that the pawn shop would not accept Stephen's books, as well as her dishing out "yellow thick" pea soup to them (begged from a nun), and then her correcting her sister Boody, who has bitterly called Simon "our father who art not in heaven"; (2) the drunken Simon trying to convince Dilly that he has no money to give her to buy some food for the family, then castigating her for not standing up straight, while Dilly pleads, "Give it up, father. . . . All the people are looking at you"; and (3) Dilly's purchase of a bit of hope in the midst of all the family squalor, *Chardenal's French Primer* (Stephen thinks, "I told her of Paris."), which leads Stephen to see his sister as drowning metaphorically, just as his mother did in fact (in her own green bile).

With great artistry, Joyce provides the antidote to possible sentimentality by his depiction of Haines, Mulligan, and (later) Master Patrick Dignam, son of the deceased. The priggish Haines has decided that Stephen suffers from a "fixed idea," an obsession; Mulligan plays along with his facile companion, telling him that it was the Church that ruined Stephen's mind with its doctrine of hellfire. Haines agrees, then ruminates that the ancient Celtic tradition does not admit of an afterlife of punishment. The obnoxious little Patrick Dignam tries as hard as he can to feel some compassion for his dead father, but he can think seriously only that he may get his name in the paper, that he will have a vacation from school, and that he might be lionized by his classmates for a time. And, despite everything, he just *cannot* get his obstreperous shirt collar to stay down!

Chapter 11:   The Sirens

This episode begins just after the 3:30 P.M. opening of the bar at the Ormond Hotel and ends at about 4:30 P.M., with the exit of Bloom and the reappearance of the blind stripling, the piano tuner, announced by the tapping sounds of his cane, who has come to retrieve the tuning fork which he had earlier left behind. Parallels with the *Odyssey* are very broad in this chapter. In Homer's epic, Odysseus stuffs his men's ears with wax so that they will not be seduced by the songs of the mermaids, who induce sailors to smash their ships on the deadly coastal rocks. Odysseus, however, wanting to hear the noted songs himself, has his men tie him to the mast and orders them to ignore him, even if he commands them to release him. The sirens here are Lydia Douce and Mina Kennedy, two barmaids, and an unappetizing prostitute that Bloom (as Ulysses) evades at the end of the episode. The most interesting parallel in this chapter with the episode in Homer's epic, however, is not the sirens themselves; it is the intoxicating power of music, whether it be sung by old men who wish to drown the memories of their failures in sentimental melodies that exalt Irish national failures or whether it is music that is heard by a middle-aged man (Bloom), who traces in the lyrics his own failures as a father and as a husband, and who will, during the course of this chapter, lose his wife to another man.

In "The Sirens," Joyce applies the intricate techniques of musical composition to literature – that is, at the beginning of the episode, he sets up a number of themes or motifs, approximately fifty-seven of them, that are interwoven and expanded throughout this chapter. "Bronze by gold," for example, refers to the bronze-haired Miss Douce and the golden-haired Miss Kennedy. "Chips" in the third line of the chapter alludes to Simon Dedalus's habit of "picking chips off one of his rocky thumbnails," noted a few pages later. "Jingle jingle jaunted jingling" is an aural prefiguration of Boylan's mare-drawn trip to 7 Eccles Street to meet Molly. The "Deepsounding. Do, Ben, do" foreshadows Ben Dollard's rendition of "The Croppy Boy" near the chapter's end, and Molly once said that the hefty Ben had a fine "barreltone" voice; in addition, the "Wait while you wait. Hee Hee" looks forward to Bloom's thoughts about Pat the waiter: "Pat is a waiter who waits while you wait. Hee hee hee hee" (as a parallel, Bloom, unable to stop the cuckolding by Boylan, is also one who will passively wait until Boylan and Molly have finished having sex).

The two main sources of musical allusions in this chapter, both reflecting Bloom's dire situation, are, first, the opera *Martha*, by the German composer von Flotow, and, second, the street ballad, mentioned previously, "The Croppy Boy," written during the second half of the nineteenth century to celebrate the Irish rebellion against the British in 1798. *Martha* concerns the deep love of Lionel for the heroine of the opera, who, unknown to him, is really the titled Lady Harriet Durham, maid of honor to Queen Anne of England. Lionel loses his mind because of the grief which he suffers when he must part from "Martha" (Lady Harriet), but his sanity is restored at the end of the opera, and he marries his beloved "Martha." *Martha*, operatically, is always associated with its most melodic song; it contains the Irish folk song " 'Tis the Last Rose of Summer." In *Ulysses*, Martha, of course, suggests Martha Clifford, for Miss Clifford is also a woman in disguise; Lionel, in another parallel, suggests Leopold Bloom, who "loses" Molly at just past 4:00 P.M., but he, in contrast, may not live happily ever again with her. Ironically, when Bloom hears Simon Dedalus singing, he realizes that his true love is Molly, *not* Martha, and the pathos is increased by Molly's incipient forsaking of him.

Of even greater importance in *Ulysses* as a means of defining Bloom's plight (and Stephen's) is the song "The Croppy Boy," a song which relates how a farm boy was executed by the British. The young Irish lad, on his way to fight the English, stops to have his confession heard by "Father Green." He walks through a lonely hall to find him, and after telling the "priest" that his father and "loving brothers all" have fallen in combat, he says: "I alone am left of my name and race." Then, as one of the childish sins which he confesses, he says that he "passed the churchyard one day in haste,/ And forgot to pray for . . . [his] mother's rest." The priest, it turns out, is a "yeoman captain" in disguise; as a result, the lad is forthwith hanged. (Note the disguise parallel and that, earlier, Joyce emphasized Stephen's agony because of his refusing to pray at the bedside of his dying mother.)

Although Bloom thinks that the Irish lad in the ballad must have been a bit thick not to have seen, even in a darkened setting, that he was talking to an *English* captain, he is moved by the fact that the boy is the last of his race: "I too, last my race. . . . No son. Rudy," Bloom says later in the chapter. Resembling the farm boy, Bloom leaves "unblessed" from the Ormond. In addition, "The Croppy Boy," with its fictitious Father Green, suggests in a physical, a political, and in a moral sense the "false father" theme of the novel. The croppy boy, as noted, is a surrogate of Stephen Dedalus, who also "forgot" – in a sense, however, Stephen *cannot* forget that he refused – to pray for a dead mother; Stephen will also be temporarily "adopted" by a father, Bloom, in this novel's last chapters. Finally, the singing of the ballad, which deals with betrayal, corresponds with Boylan's entrance into Bloom's home. The cuckolding of Bloom also suggests Peter's betrayal of Christ, as Boylan's cocksureness is literally and metaphorically recorded at the crucial moment of sexual conquest: "Cockcarracarra."

Bloom's movements, as they often do in *Ulysses*, suggest his loneliness, his isolation, and his tragic-comic situation – a situation whose sometimes pathetic depths are assuaged by Bloom's balance and common sense. Bloom passes by the Ormond Hotel carrying *Sweets of Sin* under his arm, and Lydia Douce, inside the hotel, cries: "O greasy eyes! Imagine being married to a man like that. . . ." (Since the word "greasy" is pronounced "grace-y" in Dublin, Bloom is, vocally, paralleled here as a Christ figure.) After buying stationery at Daly's to write to Martha Clifford (continuing a hollow relationship), Bloom, just after seeing a poster with a mermaid on it (another Homeric parallel), observes Boylan for the third time in the novel. But afraid to act and afraid not to act, Bloom follows Boylan into the Ormond, where he observes him without being seen.

Inside the hotel, Bloom's position is further isolated. He sits in the dining room and is thus cut off from the camaraderie (albeit superficial) and the singing at the bar. In order to hide himself further from Boylan, he chooses to eat dinner with another outcast, Richie Goulding, whom Stephen had contemplated visiting in "Proteus." "Uncle Richie" has been ruined by drink. Like Bloom, he too is subservient, and even though his brother-in-law, Simon, no longer speaks to him, Goulding admires Mr. Dedalus's voice. Goulding is so inconsequential (so thoroughly an "outcast" and a nobody) that Bloom is able to write his perfunctory letter to Martha while sitting with him, symbolically covering his uninspired jottings with the *Freeman*, yet trying to convince Richie that he is answering an ad. In the meantime, the snapped rubberband that Bloom has been playing with has its parallel with Bloom's broken relationship with Molly, and the blotted letter to Martha prefigures the end of that relationship. (Also, Bloom, who never sees matters in terms of either/or – that is, he never sees things in terms of black and white – doesn't sign the letter, and he disguises his writing by using Greek *e*'s.) Towards the conclusion of this chapter, Joyce explicitly defines Bloom's isolation: "Under the sandwichbell lay on a bier of bread one last, one lonely, last sardine of summer. Bloom alone." One is reminded here that the fish is a frequent literary symbol of Christ.

Whatever sentimentality there might be in Joyce's portrait of Bloom, presented in "The Sirens," it is countered by the comic corrective of the protagonist's breaking wind at the end of the episode; this occurs as he reads the last, noble words of the martyred Irish patriot,

Robert Emmet, found on Emmet's picture in the window of the shop of the antique dealer Lionel Marks: "When my country takes her place among the nations of the earth then and not till then, let my epitaph be written. I have done." ("Lionel," the name of the antique dealer, is an echo again of the opera *Martha*.) Bloom's (and Joyce's) "Pprrpffrrppfff. *Done*" implies a respect for life over death, for the reality of emotions deeply felt over empty political rhetoric, whether it be found in "The Croppy Boy" or in Emmet's "windy" words before his death.

Chapter 12: The Cyclops

This chapter begins just before 5:00 P.M. and takes place in Barney Kiernan's pub, to which Bloom has come to meet with Martin Cunningham so that the two men can proceed on to Paddy Dignam's residence in Sandymount in order to discuss the deceased man's life insurance policy with the bereaved family. The chapter ends with Bloom, Cunningham, Jack Power, and the Orangeman, Mr. Crofton (in Cunningham's carriage) escaping from the Citizen-cyclops. The Citizen-cyclops of Kiernan's pub is modeled upon the ardent Irish nationalist Michael Cusack, who sought to revive Gaelic sports in Ireland as a reaction against England, and Kiernan's pub becomes, metaphorically, the Homeric cave in which Odysseus and his men were imprisoned by the cannibalistic giant cyclops of Greek myth.

Other parallels with the *Odyssey* are quite explicit and determine several of this episode's motifs. In Homer's epic, the cyclops, Polyphemus, who devoured some of Odysseus's men, was, of course, one-eyed. He was also an anarchist, as were the other cyclopes in Homer's legendary country. Odysseus escaped the cyclops by getting him drunk on wine; after the monster had fallen into a deep slumber, Odysseus blinded him with a fiery stake. Odysseus and his remaining men then left the cave by latching onto the undersides of the cyclops' sheep. Since Odysseus had told Polyphemus that his name was No-Man, the giant received only ridicule from his cohorts when they asked the blinded hulk who had gored out his eye. They reasoned that because "no man" had done the deed, then the gods must be punishing Polyphemus; for that reason, they left him to an uncertain fate. As departed from the country of the cyclopes, Odysseus made the mistake of taunting the blind cyclops, who hurled a large rock at the departing voyagers. He missed Odysseus and his men, but Polyphemus asked his father, Poseidon, to curse the crew, and because Poseidon was the god of the seas, Odysseus was forced to wander for many extra years before he finally returned to Ithaca.

Many readers of Joyce's *Ulysses*, approaching the book unaided, should understand immediately that this chapter is, first of all, filled with many references to long, cylindrical objects, similar to the red-hot, stave-like weapon which Odysseus used to blind his captor. For example, the anonymous narrator of this chapter tells of almost being blinded by a street cleaner's "gear"; later, Bloom, while rejecting a drink, accepts a cigar; still later, he almost burns his fingers with it. More important, however, than these visual parallels of the Homeric stake is Joyce's clever technique of literary expansion—that is, his vision for this chapter encompasses other thin, long objects, phallic and otherwise. Bloom, for example, explains "scientifically" why hanged men undergo sexual erections at the moment of execution. J. J. O'Molloy, likewise metaphorically, speaks of the Nelson policy as "putting your blind eye to the telescope"; old Mr. Verschoyle has a long, thin ear trumpet, and the famous interpolation about trees (midway in the chapter) becomes particularly phallic, especially when coupled with the offhand reference to "Deadwood Dicks."

Closely allied to this stake motif is the "eye" metaphor, which is, of course, the more significant of the two. Joyce's main point in this episode is to satirize those people who, like the cyclops, see things (think about things) with only *one* eye—that is, those people who operate with a limited vision of the world, those who are partially, or wholly, intellectually "blind." Joyce's alcoholic and extremely anti-Semitic Fenian, for example, is obsessed with hatred for Britain. In his drunken rage, he distorts Bloom's personality and so thoroughly exasperates Joyce's protagonist that, for the first time in *Ulysses*, Bloom firmly erects his self-esteem and asserts his true nature. Likewise, the symbolic cyclops in this chapter, like his prototype, is not only chauvinistic but he is also a real phoney. As the spiteful but clever, anonymous narrator asserts, this "cyclops" has reason to fear a patriotic Irishman because of his shady dealings in the eviction of an Irish family.

Thus *eyes* predominate in "The Cyclops." Generally, the "villains" (or incompetents) are described as being one-eyed; the protagonist, in contrast, is described as having two eyes, or at least as being "cod-eyed"—that is, as being "Godeyed." Thus, the Citizen-cyclops is first seen rubbing his hand in his eye, and at the end of the episode, he misses hitting Bloom with the biscuit tin (a parallel to Polyphemus's rock) which he hurls because he is blinded by the sun (here, there is a possible parallel of Bloom's being the son of God).

In "The Cyclops," Joyce also intersperses the limited actions of the chapter with over thirty interpolations which satirize various forms of pretentiousness: literary style, national aspirations, sports reporting, mincing gestures among the upper classes, and so forth. The Citizen (unnamed throughout the chapter) is described (in one of Joyce's well-known "catalogues") as a sort of prehistoric Irish warrior and, in addition, he is adorned with the trappings and tribal images of such historical personages as Captain Nemo, Goliath, Dante Alighieri, the Queen of Sheba, Lady Godiva, and so forth. A word of praise for Bloom (by Joe) as being a humane person elicits a paragraph from the Citizen about the hen, Black Liz, that anticipates the marmalady (Joyce's term) style of the Nausicaa Episode. Later, the mention of the (fictitious) Keogh-Bennett fight evokes the worst of trite expressions—blood becomes "lively claret"—and Keogh, an "Irish gladiator." In addition, Cunningham's innocuous "God bless all here . . ." occasions a most elaborate procession to Kiernan's pub, in which the principals mainly become "saints"—that is, Bloom is seen as "S. Leopold"; the rest all become "martyrs, virgins and confessors. . . ."

Joyce structures "The Cyclops" by inculcating an ever-deepening sense of darkness, hatred, and violence, which inevitably leads up to the climactic confrontation between Bloom and the Citizen. The somewhat jaded patrons of Kiernan's pub contrast sharply with the semi-inebriated but warmly nostalgic drinkers in "The Sirens." Thus, "The Cyclops," although it takes place during the day, is really one of the so-called night parts of *Ulysses* and, as such, leads artistically to the later chapters. Kiernan's pub is indeed a sinister cave, and its denizen, the Citizen, is markedly different from his counterpart in the previous chapter, a man who is also ruined by drink—Uncle Richie Goulding. The narrator's syphilitic urination typifies with Joycean genius the entire mood of this piece.

The episode begins with the narrator's describing to Joe Hynes a trick perpetrated by the plumber Michael Geraghty, who stole from Moses Herzog but who, like Homer's Odysseus, managed to escape when he seemed to be trapped. Hynes is headed for Barney Kiernan's to meet with the Citizen to discuss a cattle traders' meeting about foot and mouth disease, and the narrator accompanies him. Inside the pub, they confront the ferocious dog, Garryowen (who does *not* belong to the Citizen, incidentally). The tone of nastiness in the chapter is augmented by Alf Bergan, who callously points out the eccentric Denis Breen, who is pursuing the libel suit over the telegram he received: "U.P.: up."

The deepening sense of gloom, the feeling that things are not all right at Kiernan's, is increased by the ensuing conversation. Alf does not know that Paddy Dignam is dead: "Sure I'm after seeing him not five minutes ago . . . as plain as a pikestaff" (another long, thin, phallic image); similarly, Bob Doran's judgment that Christ must be a "ruffian" to take poor "Willy" Dignam draws an admonition from the barman Terry, who will not tolerate blasphemy in the pub. Doran, too, is a menacing character. He was tricked into marriage in Joyce's short story "The Boarding House" (in *Dubliners*), and he is now on his yearly drinking binge. As a final touch, Joyce inserts Hynes's description of a letter of application for the position of hangman from H. Rumbold; with its gory implications, it does little to assuage the depressing atmosphere of the pub; instead, it emphasizes anew the sense of despair, depression, and futility.

Bloom enters the pub, as we might expect, at the wrong time, and the rest of the episode is structured upon one essential contrast: the violence of the pub participants set against the temperate attitude of Bloom, an attitude which is starkly out of place in this dark, cyclopian cavern. Bloom's entrance establishes him here again as a Christlike figure, and, through Joyce's careful choice of details, this sequence foreshadows Bloom's role at the end of the chapter as a kind of modern Elijah, a prophet unappreciated by his "people." When Bloom enters Kiernan's, he keeps his "cod's eye on the dog [Garryowen]." The Joycean equation of "dog" and "God" (spelled backwards) is underscored by Hynes's exclamation, "O Christ . . ."–although he is referring here to Rumbold's letter and *not* to Bloom, but he utters it just as Bloom "slopes in." Bloom twice refuses drinks, but he does accept the offer of a cigar (here is another parallel allusion to Odysseus's stake), and Bloom earns the name "prudent member" because of his abstemiousness.

But Bloom is not wholly a simple Christ figure, or even a mere hero figure; here, he is also a know-it-all, "Mister Knowall," and there is a slight justification in the annoyance of the drunken patrons at his lengthy explanations and tedious moralizing. Bloom explains, as was noted, the "scientific" and the "natural phenomenon" behind an erection of a hanged man, and Joyce recounts for us the sour narrator's comments to his audience-readers: "The fat heap he married is a nice old phenomenon with a back on her like a ballalley." Also, in answer to the Citizen's intemperate description of the British government's barbaric treatment of its sailors, Bloom further rouses the ire of the cyclops by asking "Isn't discipline the same everywhere?"; later, Bloom enunciates a typically passivistic commonplace: "Force, hatred, history, all that. That's not life for men and women, insult and hatred." Bloom, unlike the cyclops, sponsors love: "I mean the opposite of hatred."

But if this chapter portrays one of Bloom's major faults – that is, his sentimentality – it also emphasizes his heroism. Bloom is suffering the excruciating knowledge that, at this very time, Boylan is cuckolding him (starting at 4:30 P.M.); yet he persists in his errand of mercy for the Dignam family. He desperately tries to divert the conversation from the tricky Boylan to the virtues of lawn tennis (an "English" game and therefore inimical to Irish nationalists). Boylan, however, is so much on his mind that he misspeaks "wife's admirers" for "wife's advisers." He also passively suffers the Citizen's comments about a dishonored wife's bringing ruin to Ireland, sentiments expressed (ironically) by the pro-British Deasy in "Nestor," and he voices compassion for Mrs. Breen – only to have the Citizen call Denis a "half and half," a judgment which the cyclops means to be applied to Bloom.

Bloom's business affairs are equally frustrating. Hynes is spending the money which he owes to Bloom on drinks. And Nannetti, Bloom learns, is leaving for the House of Commons without deciding anything about the Keyes ad.

Yet, it is here, in "The Cyclops," that Joyce exhibits the true heroism of Bloom; for a few brief moments, the put-upon comic hero, having had enough, fights back by *asserting* his *Jewishness*. He begins to become irritated when the Citizen, in response to Bloom's insistence that Ireland is his nation, spits an oyster into a corner. Bloom becomes angry for the first time in *Ulysses*: "And I belong to a race too . . . that is hated and persecuted. Also now. This very moment. This very instant."

After Bloom leaves the drinkers for a moment to find Cunningham, the Citizen and his cronies, now thoroughly intoxicated, sponsor the silly belief that Bloom won a bet on Throwaway, but will not stand them to a round of drinks. They accuse him (wrongly, using

Joyce's irony) of "defrauding widows and orphans." When Bloom returns to find that Martin Cunningham has been in Kiernan's while Bloom has been looking for him in the courthouse, the action proceeds to its conclusion. In answer to the anti-Semitic slurs of the dropsical Polyphemus-like character of the cyclops, Bloom (like Odysseus in Homer's epic) cannot help but retort: "Your God was a jew. Christ was a jew like me." And although the empty biscuit box thrown by the Citizen causes a mock heroic seismic disturbance, it has no more effect than Polyphemus's boulder. Bloom escapes down Little Green Street and is assumed, metaphorically and linguistically, into Heaven. The motif of the throwaway that announced Elijah's coming has now run its course.

Chapter 13: Nausicaa

This episode takes place at around 8:00 P.M. on Sandymount Strand, the same shore where Stephen had earlier that morning contemplated the meaning of life's changes in "Proteus." Bloom has just come from visiting the Dignam family (in Sandymount), and "Nausicaa" provides him with a "relief" from the unpleasantness of Barney Kiernan's pub in "The Cyclops," and it also furnishes him respite from the somber atmosphere of the bereaved Dignam household. Joyce gains continuity with the previous episode, "The Cyclops," despite the time differential by continuing several motifs from that chapter, the most prominent of which is the *arc*. The rising and falling of the biscuit tin which was flung by the Citizen is reflected in the various ascents and declines in "Nausicaa": for example, Gerty MacDowell's tempting leg, the Roman candle's rise and climactic explosion from the Mirus Bazaar, and the swinging censer of the church benediction – all of these risings and fallings lead up to and down from the simultaneous orgasms of Gerty and Bloom. Also, the form of the episode is as simple as its style (Joyce called it – perhaps knowingly – a "marmalady" style, a sticky style). The first part of the episode deals with Gerty; the second, with Bloom and his ruminations.

Parallels with Homer are not difficult to recognize. Odysseus, washed ashore on the land of the Phaeacians, was awakened from sleep when he was struck by a ball misthrown by Princess Nausicaa and her friends; the resourceful and beautiful young girl had come to the shore to play and wash some clothing. Not nonplussed by the appearance of a naked stranger, Nausicaa told the hapless, storm-tossed wanderer to go to her father's palace to receive succor. Gerty (Joyce's Nausicaa) aids Ulysses-Bloom by enticing him into the sexual respite provided by auto-eroticism, an act which he has been postponing until now. She also parallels the unmarried Nausicaa of Homer because marriage is much on Gerty's mind, especially after her breakup with her steady boyfriend, Reggie Wylie (a parallel here with Bloom's "loss" of Molly). In addition, Nausicaa in Homer's epic performed the menial task of washing her family's linens; Joyce's heroine, however, causes Bloom to (ironically) "dirty" his clothes by masturbating. Gerty is also compared to the Blessed Mother, and Mary's colors, especially blue, appear throughout the episode. Mary, of course, is the Catholics' Refuge of Sinners and, to them, a last resort for bewildered and perplexed mankind – in this instance, Bloom.

Joyce, in "Nausicaa," however, is doing much more than satirizing cheap, sentimental romance fiction: in this episode, he reveals the hidden side of Irish womanhood, as he will also later do in "Penelope," in Molly's soliloquy. In fact, in two significant ways, Gerty foreshadows Molly: Gerty, as does Molly, pleads for more understanding from men, especially priests, who hear women's intimate confessions; and Gerty and Molly are compared many times by Joyce to the Blessed Virgin.

Gerty knows exactly what she is doing in "seducing" Bloom – the dark and mournful foreign stranger – as she leads him to a moment of communication, albeit an ultimately unproductive one. She is aware of the allure of her transparent stockings: "Her woman's instinct told her that she had raised the devil in him. . . ." She finds a co-conspirator in her friend Cissy Caffrey, who goes to ask her "uncle Peter" what time it is. Gerty has been told in the past about men's passions by Bertha Supple; thus, Gerty is very much aware of why Bloom keeps his hands in his pockets as he watches her display her underclothing. In short, she is scarcely the "fair unsullied soul" that Stephen saw calling to him at a climactic moment towards the end of Book Four of A Portrait. Stephen interpreted his "Pagan Mary" as beckoning him to the freedom of Europe; but in Ulysses, Joyce effectively portrays here the limitations of human nature, as well as its exalted moments. It was, in fact, Joyce's revelation of the darker passions of repressed womanhood, as well as its "blasphemous" commingling of sex and religion that led to the suppression of Ulysses (in its serial format) by the New York Society for the Prevention of Vice in 1921.

The second part of "Nausicaa," as noted, concerns Bloom's thoughts—lethargic ones, for the most part, after his sexual emission; therefore, it is of little wonder that his ruminations deal with physiological matters. He recalls his almost approaching Mrs. Clinch, whom he mistakenly took to be a prostitute, and then he recalls the occasion when he paid a girl in Meath Street to say dirty words aloud. He also recalls the romance between Molly and Mulvey, and he thinks again about the time when he made love to Molly on Howth Hill. He wonders if Boylan pays Molly for sex, and, in true businesslike fashion, he estimates how much Molly is worth. He recalls the song of Boylan's about "seaside girls," the girls having become Gerty and her two friends. As usual though, Bloom is an old "stick in the mud," and his phallic "stick" being limp, he tosses his writing implement into the sand, where it sticks, literally. As the cuckoo bird at the end of "Nausicaa" indicates, Bloom, despite all his thoughts about sex, is the cuckolded one.

In addition, "Nausicaa" is cleverly related to other chapters in *Ulysses* in various other ways. For instance, Bloom notes that his watch has stopped at 4:30 P.M., the probable time of Molly's intercourse with Boylan. He pulls the sticky, semen-soiled material away from his foreskin, and his exclamation of "Ow!" reminds us of the unnamed narrator's painful, syphilitic urination in "The Cyclops." (This matter of Bloom having a foreskin has been the subject of recent scholarship; the Virag genealogy has been traced and, technically, Bloom is *not* a Jew. Thus, Bloom becomes, metaphorically, "neither fish nor fowl," paralleling his alienated social status in Dublin.) In this chapter, too, Bloom reveals that he was indeed aware of the newsboys' mimicry of his gait in "Aeolus" although once again he is able to escape into the world of imagination; here, he contemplates publishing a story in *Titbits* ("The Mystery Man on the Beach"), based on his own beach experience. He takes pride in his challenge to the Citizen in "The Cyclops": "Got my own back there." And his estimate of his sexual prowess is a somber one, which reminds the reader of Stephen's Parable of the Plums at the end of "Aeolus": "He [Boylan] gets the plums and I the plumstones."

Towards the close of "Nausicaa," Bloom draws the letters "I. . . . AM. A" on the sand, and the meaning is ambiguous. Several critics have advanced various possibilities as to Joyce's intent. Bloom *could* be the Christ who wrote an unknown message in the road to save the "woman taken in adultery." Or Bloom might be a kind of a kind of parallel to the Old Testament God: "I Am Who Am." He might also be indicating that he is not quite a full man at this point: "I am a man." Or as the Joyce scholar Fritz Senn has pointed out, Bloom's last thoughts might be of love, since *ama* is the Latin word for *love*. Certainly, Bloom's thoughts in the episode *have* been about Mrs. Purefoy, who has spent three days in labor, and whom he will visit in the next episode. At the end of the chapter, nonetheless, Bloom remains the charitable hero despite his pointless spilling of the seed that would continue his name and thus fulfill his duty as a Jew.

Chapter 14:   The Oxen of the Sun

This episode begins at about 10:00 P.M. and ends approximately an hour later. Its setting is the National Maternity Hospital in Dublin, and one of the hospital's superintendents is Dr. Andrew J. Horne, whose name is subjected to much punning by Stephen Dedalus and his friends. The physical action of the chapter is simple enough. The semi-inebriated Stephen is drinking with some of his boisterous acquaintances, some of whom are medical students, and he is also drinking with some others, such as Lenehan, who are simply hangers-on. The young men are unconcerned over the plight of Mina Purefoy, who has just passed her third full day in labor. In fact, the birth of her son during this episode elicits only a jocular response from the rowdy young men. At the beginning of "The Oxen of the Sun," Bloom visits the hospital because he is concerned about Mrs. Purefoy; after her baby has been delivered, Bloom decides to stay and watch over Stephen. Bloom's worry is evoked by both his friendship with Simon Dedalus and his fear that Stephen is dissipating his talents through drinking and lecherous associates. Towards the end of the chapter, Stephen suggests that he and his drinking friends adjourn to a pub, Burke's. There, Stephen becomes thoroughly drunk from drinking too much absinthe, which he also buys for the others, thus further reducing the meager pay that he received earlier from Mr. Deasy in "Nestor." As the chapter closes, Lynch and Stephen head for the brothel district, with Bloom referred to here as the "johnny in the black duds," where he will continue his inexpert role of the impromptu, self-appointed caretaker of Stephen. In the midst of the episode, Mulligan enters with Bannon, and the two of them discuss Bannon's liaison with Milly Bloom in Mullingar. Mulligan departs, and Stephen and Lynch, as we discover in "Circe" (Chapter 15) join Mulligan and Haines at the West-

land Row station (en route to the brothel district) at about a quarter
past eleven. Stephen and Mulligan apparently scuffle, and Stephen
hurts his hand. Stephen, however, proceeds along with Lynch to the
prostitutes, and Haines and Mulligan presumably return to the
Martello Tower. Bloom, after getting off at the wrong train stop,
must, in "Circe," catch up to Stephen in Nighttown.

The parallel with Homer, here, is broad, but is very important in
this episode. Odysseus's men, despite his warnings, slaughtered the
cattle of the sun god, Helios, and thus brought death upon themselves, leaving Odysseus as the only survivor of the voyage from
Troy. In Joyce, the "slaughter" is apparent on several levels. Literally,
the Homeric parallel is with the Kerry cows; they are suffering from
foot and mouth disease (the Deasy letter appeared in the paper this
evening – because of Stephen's influence), and these cows might well
be slaughtered in Liverpool. Of much greater concern than the
slaughter of these cattle, however, is the whole matter of birth and
death, life and its prevention. Joyce was somewhat conservative re-
garding matters of birth control, and he was dubious about anything
that might prevent the issuance of new life.

As a result, Joyce saw in the "sterile" talk of Stephen and his
friends that sterility itself was an analogy for human impotence in
general – that is, the profitless nature of man's questioning the divin-
ity, as well as the question about the decay of Ireland, etc. Mulligan,
as was demonstrated in "Telemachus" and also in "Scylla and
Charybdis," again becomes the "villain" of the piece; he is the major
spokesman for narcissistic, profitless sex. Here, he enters and hands
out cards announcing his new trade: *Mr. Malachi Mulligan, Fertiliser
and Incubator, Lambay Island.* His "mythic" plans are really about sex,
and though they are supposedly about fertility, the announcement of
his idea is followed by a page of puns about contraceptives, with
cloaks and umbrellas heading the list. Joyce's characterization of
Mulligan is stern; nor does Bloom escape unscathed: for all of his
charitable nurturing, Bloom has just spilled his seed in the preceding
episode, and we are reminded that a "habit reprehensible at puberty
is second nature and an opprobrium in middle life." Also, Bloom's
first sexual encounter, with Bridie Kelly (St. Brigid, symbolically and
ironically, is the Irish patroness of purity), was anything but fruitful,
even when its sterility is considered in sentimental, nineteenth-
century terms: "She [Bridie] dare not bear the sunnygolden babe of

day." Joyce's positive attitude about birth and life is clearly evident in the design of "The Oxen of the Sun": the nine months of gestation are marked (loosely) by the so-called nine "periods" (or stages, phases of development) of the English language, through which the plot and themes of this chapter are presented. Scholars have with some justification criticized Joyce's elaborate architectonics in this chapter, but if we consider the serious purpose which underlies Joyce's parodies, the chapter becomes much easier to comprehend. The true protagonist in "The Oxen of the Sun" is the birth process itself; in this case, Joyce focuses, along with his literal subject matter, on a matter of major concern to him: the birth of the English language. He demonstrates here (and in *Finnegans Wake*) just how fruitful the insemination has proved to be.

The language of "The Oxen of the Sun" does indeed present many difficulties for the reader – most notably in the opening pages. The first entry means simply: "Let us turn towards the sun [metaphorical] and go to Holles Street [the location of Horne's hospital]." The second entry is an invocation to the sun god (the Homeric parallel), here seen as Dr. Horne, asking that Mrs. Purefoy's baby be delivered. The third passage is the anticipated cry of a midwife as she announces the birth of a male child. The next three (lengthy) paragraphs are written in a pre-English, Latinized style, in which Joyce simply inserted praise for the Celtic nation because of its tradition of providing medical care and comfort for mothers, despite the general poverty of the country.

One should keep the simple action of this chapter at the back of the consciousness and should concentrate, instead, on Joyce's brilliant *use* of the various forms of English. The Old English tone of the language lends scope to Leopold Bloom's errand of mercy, situating him somewhere between the Wandering Jew and Beowulf: for example, consider how Joyce inserts this description of his protagonist: "Stark ruth [pity] of man his errand that him lone led till that house." Likewise, the somber thought of death in the midst of life is evoked through the old medieval morality play *Everyman*: "Look to that last end that is thy death. . . ." Later, language imitative of John Bunyan allows Joyce to define precisely the roles of Bloom ("Calmer") and Stephen ("Boasthard's"). In true Bunyan manner, the prophylactic becomes a character in its own right – that is, the "shield which was named Killchild." In the century following Bunyan's time,

Charles Lamb's essays often revolved around memories of child-hood; here, Joyce uses them as the model for Bloom's reminiscences about his own fruitless past. And still later, historically, Dickensian sentimentality, with its sugared picture of a contented mother and child, underlines the contrast between this superficial version of life and the agonizing pain that Mina Purefoy has just suffered. The nineteenth-century Gothic novel accounts for Mulligan's dramatic and chilling evocation of Haines and his black panther; and the modern slang of the closing pages of this chapter both captures the drunken antics of the principals and, on a cosmic level, predicts the breakdown of Western culture and its language.

For this reason, *Ulysses* is simultaneously a cosmic and a comic novel; especially in this chapter the fusion is evident, and often the comic spirit predominates. The very serious linguistic parodies are highly humorous. Bloom appears as a medieval knight during his visit to the hospital; we are told that on May 23, 1904, Bloom required help from Dr. Dixon to assist with a painful bee sting: "for he was sore wounded in his breast by a spear wherewith a horrible and dreadful dragon was smitten him. . . ." Bloom is also (knight-like) wearied from his travels; he is "sore of limb," having practiced (on the beach in "Nausicaa") "sometimes venery." Again, too, the obscene banter of the young men in this chapter is compared in stilted rhetorical terms to a Socratic discussion, and in the breakup of language at the chapter's close, American black slang is inserted in the pandemonium of voices – in this instance, extolling the virtues of Dignam: "Of all de darkies Massa Pat was verra best."

In "The Oxen of the Sun," though, in a few places Joyce breaks through the stage scrim filament of crafted language, and he provides stark, explicit information which is crucial to a full comprehension of *Ulysses*. For example, Stephen is truly terrified by the thunderstorm, and Bloom is unable to calm him. Stephen half-believes that the thunder is God's retort to his blasphemies (interestingly, Joyce himself was afraid of thunderstorms). Also, the cocksure Stephen of "Nestor" there defined God as a shout in the street; now, it seems as though retribution is at hand. In addition, thunder has always been associated with the Hammer of Thor, and Joyce *does* set this novel on "Thor's Day."

Finally, "The Oxen of the Sun" brings together Stephen and Bloom; this has been a meeting which Joyce has been working towards since the novel began and, even though their words do not lead to any clear communication here, the meeting does presage their discussions in subsequent chapters. Already, Joyce begins to fuse fragments of the two men's backgrounds. Bloom's memory of the four- or five-year-old Stephen, dressed in "linseywoolsey" at the get-together at Mat Dillon's (the occasion during which Bloom bested Menton at bowls) in May, 1887, is combined with sad thoughts of his own dead son, Rudy, and the "corselet of lamb's wool" that Molly knitted "for his burial." Bloom is indeed, clearly, on a search for a son, having "no manchild for an heir"; thus, he "looked upon him [Stephen] his friend's [Simon's] son. . . ."

Chapter 15:   Circe

This episode of *Ulysses* is based more loosely upon Homer's epic than are the other episodes in the novel. In Homer's *Odyssey*, Circe turned Odysseus's men into swine; Odysseus, however, never succumbed to Circe's spells. In Joyce's *Ulysses*, Circe (the symbolic female of this chapter) is Bella Cohen, and she keeps a brothel at 82 Tyrone Street Lower, in the midst of the Dublin redlight district, the district that Joyce (but not the Dubliners of 1904) calls Nighttown in *Ulysses*. Unlike Homer's hero, Bloom is not spared the debasement of Odysseus's men (and, of course, in the original, Odysseus did not undergo a transformation). Bloom *is* debased, and, significantly, this chapter initiates the subsequent cathartic effect of that debasement.

Joyce, of course, did not need Homer's epic to supply the hallucinogenic character of the events in "Circe." There are ample precedents in literature—"objective correlatives," as T. S. Eliot called them, for "objectifying" inner states of fictional characters. In Coleridge's Ancient Mariner's tale, the protagonist's spiritual desiccation is reflected in the dryness of the atmosphere at sea; likewise, the witches in *Macbeth* probably emanate from Macbeth's and Banquo's desires for power; the Faustian "Walpurgisnacht" literally records the darker, frenzied side of human passion; and *Venus in Furs*, written by Leopold von Sacher-Masoch in 1870, certainly raised psychosexual behavior to a new and startling literary art form. Clearly, though, both Homer in his *Odyssey* and Joyce in "Circe" are concerned with a universal psychological theme: the fear that expression of sexuality might well turn the participants into "animals."

In addition to examining Bloom's (and to a lesser degree, Stephen's) expressionistic visions, however, it is important to define the literal narrative of the episode; thus, for the sake of convenience, if one divides this chapter into separate parts, the first part of "Circe" concludes with Stephen's sighting of Bloom in the music room of Mrs. Cohen's establishment. At this point, Stephen turns to Bloom and says, "A time, times and half a time." This same expression is used in the Bible to account for the length of time before the Day of Judgment is to arrive. For Stephen, this "Day" occurs in "Circe" when he meets his dead mother in a vision.

The Circe Episode begins at the Mabbot Street entrance to Nighttown, and Joyce at once establishes the ethereal tone of the chapter: the pygmy woman and the gnome mentioned on the first page are undoubtedly children, but they are distorted because they are seen through the mists of Joyce's spell of enchantment. Stephen and Lynch pass close to two men, Privates Compton and Carr, and the obnoxious Carr calls Stephen a parson because of his black clothing; this foreshadows the trouble which Stephen will have with this British soldier at the close of the episode, when Carr knocks Stephen down. A whore, also mistaking Stephen, believes that the two men are Trinity College medical students: "All prick and no pence." Stephen – although it can only be surmised – is probably in Nighttown to seek out Georgina Johnson, a prostitute whom he paid once with George Russell's loan of a pound (this reference occurs in "Scylla and Charybdis").

Bloom arrives panting from his attempt to catch up with Stephen and Lynch, and he is almost run down by two cyclists and then is almost hit by a sandstrewer; this latter encounter, at least, however, cures his (Christ-like) pain in his side. Although he thinks that following Stephen is probably futile, Bloom pursues his quest since he feels that Stephen is the "best of the lot." Also, he is afraid that Stephen will lose his money, and, after all, the chase is really, according to one of Bloom's stray and unconscious thoughts, "Kismet" (fate or destiny).

In the phantasmagoric, dream-like sequences of "Circe," Bloom manages to arrive in front of Mrs. Cohen's establishment (although he thinks that he has arrived at "Mrs. Macks"). There, the whore Zoe Higgins (whose last name is the same as Bloom's mother's maiden name) tells him that the young man whom he is looking for is inside;

she then asks (note Joyce's use of irony here) if Bloom is the young man's father; significantly, Bloom "denies" his "son." Zoe ("life" in Greek) is verbose, and Bloom's response to another of her crude questions—"How's the nuts?"—lends credence to one critic's assertion that we probably know more about Bloom than about any other protagonist in literature. "Off side" is Bloom's answer, referring to his testicles. "Curiously," he says, "they are on the right. Heavier I suppose. One in a million my tailor, Mesias [note that Bloom looked for a mesial groove in the nude museum statue in "Scylla and Charybdis"] says." Zoe then takes Bloom's shriveled potato, his true *moly*, and Joyce focuses sharply here on Zoe's lips, "smeared with salve of swinefat"; clearly, Joyce is placing us in Homer's own pen of Circe.

Bloom's lewd censuring of Zoe's smoking, and Zoe's injunction that Bloom should make an impromptu oration on the subject elicit a *fantasy* that lasts over twenty pages. Zoe finally has enough: "Talk away till you're black in the face," she says, after which Bloom accompanies her into the music room of the whorehouse. He is a rather pathetic man here—truly tripping as he enters the establishment. But enter he does, to join Lynch and Stephen, and the "antlered rack" is a reminder of his being cuckolded by Boylan.

The second part of "Circe" climaxes in the most important moment of the entire novel: Stephen smashes his ashplant against the whorehouse chandelier in defiance of his mother's attempts to foist upon him an increased sense of guilt in order to lead him back to the Church. As he smashes the symbolic "light," he screams *"Nothung!"* "Nothung," significantly and again symbolically, is the sword of Siegfried, the hero of Wagner's magnificent operatic rendering of myth—*The Ring of the Niebelung*. Clearly, Joyce was more deeply influenced by Wagner than most critics have guessed. In his play, *Exiles*, for example, Joyce uses as the name of his protagonist "Richard"; he calls him "Richard Rowan," and "Richard" was Wagner's first name, and the "rowan" is, in fact, an ash tree, the substance from which Stephen's walking stick is made, and it is also the tree from which Siegfried's heroic sword was buried for many years before it was finally wrenched free. The language that Joyce uses in describing the (literally) minor damage to the chandelier indicates that Joyce wants us to focus not on it, but on Stephen's rebellion against his mother's apparition; this is the high point of the novel (at least as far as Stephen is concerned): *"Time's livid final flame leaps and, in the following darkness, ruin of all space, shattered glass and toppling masonry."*

Many factors, carefully delineated by Joyce in "Circe," account for Stephen's hallucinations and for his act of rebellion. His blurred vision, for example, is caused by his earlier breaking of his eyeglasses, and his hand lacks power because it was injured during his fight with Mulligan. Stephen has waltzed feverishly with the whores on a stomach which is empty of food, but which is full of alcohol. These are the physical claims on him; the metaphysical and spiritual claims are embodied in his mother – and she makes many claims on him: Stephen holds the first-born status in his family; there are memories of his mother's reassuring him when he was lonely and away from his friends; there is her insistence that he kneel down and *pray* for her suffering soul, despite his *non serviam* delivered to God; and, finally, there is Stephen's recollection of his singing to his mother as she lay dying. Stephen is also reminded of Mulligan's recurring statement that it was he, Stephen, who killed his mother (who is now "beastly dead") because he refused to pray at her bedside.

Part Two of "Circe," then, includes Stephen's "dark night of the soul," as it were, but it is no less a trial for Bloom, for it is a night in which all of his own secret obsessions are laid bare.

Bloom's masochistic binge begins with the entrance of the swinish Bella Cohen. It ends (temporarily) with the "Bip!" of his back trouser button, a noise which recalls him to reality. At this point, he turns on Bella (who has now resumed her real name in Joyce's text; during the masochistic session, she was referred to in the Latin, masculine equivalent, *Bello*), and Bloom begins to point out her physical flaws. This temporary return to the conscious world permits Bloom to safeguard Stephen's money, for Bella Cohen would certainly have cheated him. Unfortunately, Stephen does not appreciate what Bloom is doing for him, even when Bloom says, "This is yours." Bloom's victory and his "saving" of Stephen are short-lived, however, for with the appearance of Boylan's avatar, Bloom begins imagining that he is watching Blazes Boylan make unbridled (or bridled, possibly) love to Molly.

This major masochistic streak in Bloom's psyche has drawn much attention from Joycean critics; some find it humorous, some lurid, and some feel that it reveals universal traits which are buried in all of us. Certainly, Bloom's psyche is composed of many and varied elements: foot fetishes, transvestism, coprophilia (an abnormal attraction to fecal matter), and guilt over the picture of the naked nymph that hangs over the Blooms' bed–to name just four bizarre elements. But Joyce obviously felt a need to include these diverse, exotic components of Bloom's subconscious mind if he were to portray a complete, *individuated* character. There *had* to be a "Circe" chapter in this novel to release them, to let them all emerge, for Bloom's second drink would not have accounted for all of the revelations, contrary to his opinion. Also, the sexual nightmare that Joyce portrays provides a catharsis for Bloom, permitting him to capably help Stephen during the ending chapters of *Ulysses*. Finally, Joyce in "Circe" is close to certain theories of Freud in his belief that dreams are purgations.

The third and final part of "Circe" begins with Stephen's dashing out of the bordello and with Bloom (temporarily purged of guilt) revealing a side of himself that we have seen before only once–at the end of "The Cyclops," when he talked back, defiantly, to the Citizen. Here, however, he does not *run*; instead, he stays and cares for Stephen, braving the soldiers *and* the police. He is truly angry with Bella for wanting ten shillings for the broken lamp, and he threatens her with revealing the fact that she is supporting her son at Oxford with money gained through prostitution; finally, he forces her to accept a shilling as payment for the damaged fixture. Also, it is Bloom who stays by Stephen when Lynch (a Judas figure) deserts the lad and when Corny Kelleher implies that Sandycove is too far to go to bring Stephen home.

Stephen's trouble with Carr is occasioned by his symbolic comment, "But in here it is I must kill the priest and the king." Carr thinks that Stephen is threatening to assassinate Edward VII; he will not listen to Bloom's entreaties that Stephen has been drinking absinthe. Actually, Stephen is repeating the adage that Ireland is a captive of the double tyrants of the Roman Catholic Church and Britain. More symbolism is also apparent in Carr's attack on Stephen just after Bloom has said that Stephen is "incapable": the blow represents, symbolically, English oppression of a nearly defenseless Ireland.

Despite the somber tone of part three of this chapter, however, the section is filled with many humorous overtones and subtle ironies–even apart from the delightfully farcical apparitions that follow upon Stephen's priest and king statement. Kelleher, for instance, brought to Nighttown someone who had lost on the Gold Cup race, and this person might *possibly* be Boylan. This would be an incredible irony, especially when seen against Molly's recollections of

Blazes' sexual proclivities in "Penelope." And poor Bloom, despite all of his Good Samaritan doings, is misjudged (again): Kelleher thinks that Bloom has been visiting the prostitutes for his *own* uses: "Not for old stagers like myself and yourself."

"Circe" ends with a terrifying vision – the most terrifying vision of all the visions in this chapter, and Bloom, despite all that has happened to him in this episode, must suffer even more grief. His dead son Rudy appears to him as he would have been – had he lived, and although Bloom's image is an idealized one, it is terribly unnerving. It is, however, touchingly real and moving. We realize anew that Bloom is a marvelous composite of all the elements that make up mankind. His capacity for wonder and beauty is dramatically revealed here in the harrowing apparition of little Rudy, the Lamb of the World.

Chapter 16: Eumaeus

In Homer's epic, Odysseus meets with the faithful and hospitable swineherd Eumaeus after Odysseus has returned to Ithaca; shortly thereafter, Odysseus joins with Telemachus and slaughters Penelope's suitors. In Joyce's novel, a coffeehouse which is said to be run by Skin-the-Goat (James) Fitzharris provides a symbolic place for Bloom and Stephen to chat before the two men return to Bloom's house in the next chapter. (Fitzharris, one should recall, drove the decoy car after the Phoenix Park Murders, discussed prominently in "Aeolus.") The Homeric parallel also reinforces two other themes in the episode: first, the motif of disguises and the imagery of the wanderer's return; no one knows whether the returned sailor "W. B. Murphy" really bears that name, or whether, like Bloom and Odysseus, he actually is going to return to a wife whom he has not seen for several years. And who knows whether Parnell, like Bloom, will ever "return" – that is, were there really only *stones* buried in Parnell's casket? And, more important to this narrative, will Bloom be able to return in any meaningful way to Molly?

After the excesses of Nighttown, Bloom and Stephen, at about 1:00 A.M., walk to Fitzharris's cabman's shelter to imbibe a non-alcoholic beverage. On the way, Stephen meets the dissipated Corley (a sponger from "Two Gallants" in *Dubliners*); he lends the fellow some money and tells him that there will be a job available at Deasy's school (this is Stephen's own position; he will be leaving the school).

Once inside the shelter, Bloom and Stephen discuss many subjects: Murphy's wanderings, the sensuality of Gibraltar women, nationalism, and religion, to name a few. Bloom also reads a copy of the *Telegraph*; it contains the mistakes caused, in part, by the misunderstandings in "Hades." After considering and weighing the consequences of bringing Stephen home, and with misgivings (Bloom is afraid that Molly will complain), Bloom does decide finally to bring Stephen home with him ("It's not far. Lean on me."). Thus, the two start out towards 7 Eccles Street.

Bloom's motives for helping Stephen are mostly altruistic. In "Hades," when Bloom saw Stephen, Stephen was alone—that is, he was without his *"fidus Achates"*—the "cad," Mulligan. In "Eumaeus," the recurrence of this same phrase indicates that Bloom is indeed filling an immediate need of Stephen's. Joyce makes it clear that Bloom is helping Stephen by warning him to avoid the robust but superficial Buck Mulligan. Mulligan "contributes the humorous element," it is true, but Bloom feels that Mulligan cannot be trusted. Bloom observed more than Stephen could when the medical students were drinking in "The Oxen of the Sun" chapter. Bloom believes that Mulligan may have put something into Stephen's drink. Clearly, Bloom feels compassion for Stephen; he thinks that Stephen is a bright young man, recently returned from Paris—a young man who may not "have it all together yet." In Stephen's eyes, Bloom sees the eyes of Stephen's sisters and father. He thinks that it is a pity that "a young fellow blessed with an allowance of brains . . . should waste his valuable time with profligate women. . . ." And, after all, Bloom brought home a dog with a lame paw (there is a parallel here with Stephen's injured hand); thus, why not do it again—even though Molly might become irate?

Bloom acts basically because of his innate charity (making him once again a twentieth-century Christ figure), but his motives are mixed. A careful reading of "Eumaeus" dispels the trite notion that Bloom is either a simple plaster saint or a merely farcical protagonist. His assessment of Stephen's personality, for example, as well as his assessment of Stephen's talents is shrewd, and often in "Eumaeus," Bloom imagines how Stephen can be used to his (Bloom's) advantage. As a writer, Stephen could help Bloom advertise the new opera company which he is conceiving in his imagination by "providing puffs in the local papers," since Stephen is undoubtedly a "fellow with a bit of bounce. . . ." In one sense, we should realize that Bloom is willing to take Stephen home, to spend a few pennies on him because of possible benefits that may come from Bloom's cultivating "the acquaintance of someone of no uncommon calibre who could provide food for reflection. . . ." In other words, the mercantilistic, advertising side of Bloom will sacrifice some "food and lodging" to acquire from Stephen some "food for thought." Then, too, Bloom might find in the meeting with Stephen enough material to publish in *Titbits*, in the manner of the vaunted Philip Beaufoy: "*My Experiences*, let us say, *in a Cabman's Shelter*." Or perhaps since Stephen has his father's voice, Bloom might profit from Stephen's fine tenor renditions. Finally, Bloom offers one of the best summaries of Stephen's character ever penned: "His initial impression was that he was a bit standoffish or not over effusive but it grew on him someway." This "impression" of Stephen is exactly what many readers of *Ulysses* have throughout the novel.

Sadly, though, there are too many differences between Stephen and Bloom in order for them to be truly compatible and complementary, and "Eumaeus" contains the seeds of the dissolution of their temporary friendship, which will end after June 17. The gap between these two men is ultimately too great, and at the end of the novel, we are left with only Molly's thoughts as Stephen (now usurping the role of the Chaplinesque "little tramp") wanders off to an unknown destiny. Joyce makes it clear that—even as Bloom and Stephen enter the shelter—*misunderstanding* is the key to this episode. Bloom praises the Italian spoken by a group of people standing around an ice cream cart, and Stephen deflates his adorational "a beautiful language" by explaining: "They were haggling over money." Bloom again points out the dangers of prostitution (the spread of venereal disease), and Stephen asserts that the Irish people have sold much more than their bodies—he means, of course, their souls. Also, Bloom's point that Shakespeare's plays may have been written by Bacon is pathetic, following, as it does, Stephen's highly abstruse discussion of Shakespeare in "Scylla and Charybdis." Again, Bloom's insistence that in his new, proposed socialistic state everyone must work falls wide of the mark, and he hurriedly explains that Stephen would be acceptable too, since writing poetry could be defined as "labor," of a sort. Bloom's assurance that both the "brain and the brawn" belong to Ireland elicits merely Stephen's enigmatic retort: "Ireland must be important because it belongs to me."

It is in matters of religion, though, that Bloom and Stephen are furthest apart, philosophically and spiritually. Ironically, Bloom thinks that Stephen is a "good catholic"; he states and restates this judgment, summing it up finally in the statement: "orthodox as you are." However, it is the word "simple" that Stephen uses in discussing the human soul that clearly delineates the contrast between the two men. Bloom responds: "Simple? I shouldn't think that is the proper word." What Stephen has in mind is the scholastic definition of "simple" – that is, having no parts. God is simple; so is the soul. But Bloom just does not have the intellectual capacity to appreciate such complexities; he is too mired in the real world of money and politics – as he always will be.

Joyce's theme of *wandering*, of people destined never to join significantly but, instead, to move through webs of artifice, is epitomized in the character of W. B. Murphy – if, indeed, that is his true name. The red-bearded Murphy, who, with his typically Irish blather and blarney, resembles the clever narrator of "The Cyclops," is a drunken, belligerent misfit weaving his life around a tissue of lies. In many ways, Murphy typifies the worst traits of the archetypal Irishman, but, with his colorful personality, he has an abundance of compensating, attractive qualities. Here, Murphy has come from the three-master ship *Rosevean*, the ship that Stephen saw in "Proteus," and one wonders if the bricks which the vessel carries will lead to any future foundation (one is reminded of the stones, again, that are supposed to be in Parnell's coffin – instead of his body – and one is also reminded of the fact that Joyce modeled the amorphous hero of *Finnegans Wake* upon a drunken hod carrier). Murphy, another mock-heroic avatar of the returned Odysseus, is about to reintroduce himself to the wife that he has not seen in seven years. Bloom thinks of various returned heroes from fiction, and he cannot help projecting his own doubts onto his vision of the upcoming reunion: what if they don't want the returnee any more, and what is really Murphy's name, anyway? Is it possibly *"Señor A. Boudin,"* as the postcard seems to imply?

Even more effectively than Murphy's own personal myths, however, Parnell's story better depicts Bloom's lonely desperation and his status as a wanderer with only a tenuous Ithaca to return to. Parnell, according to the pundits, was destroyed by a woman, Kitty O'Shea, his mistress. Like Molly, Kitty (the wife of Captain O'Shea) was a "fine lump of a woman . . ." and during the O'Shea divorce trial, Parnell became a laughing stock when it was revealed that he was seen scrambling down a ladder from Kitty's room in his night-clothes; in the next episode, the keyless Bloom will similarly have to scramble to get into his own home. What bothers Bloom about the retelling of the Parnell story in "Eumaeus" is "the blatant jokes of the cabmen . . . who passed it all off as a jest. . . ." To Bloom, who lives only in an imaginary sexual world (either with Martha Clifford or masturbating on the beach in "Nausicaa"), Parnell is a truly sexual, athletic hero, one who literally died for love. Bloom, quite naturally, probably envisions himself as the impotent Captain O'Shea, who, historically, agreed to ignore his wife's infidelity with Parnell (as Bloom is doing with Boylan) until O'Shea was convinced by a number of politicians that Parnell *had* to be disgraced and therefore lose office. And, after all, Parnell did thank Bloom once for picking up his hat, a marked contrast to Menton's treatment of Bloom in "Hades," when Bloom graciously pointed out a dint in the hat.

Throughout this episode, Joyce infuses a sense of exhaustion, emptiness, and futile wandering. The syntax contributes immensely to this effect, as Joyce fills the chapter with lengthy, unfinished sentences, creating an atmosphere of vast attenuation, artifice, and especially a feeling of tiredness. And in the midst of all this, the dissipated Corley presents a warning of what Stephen might become: "His friends had all deserted him." The Simon Dedalus that Murphy describes is almost certainly not Stephen's father, but rather a sharp-shooter who traveled with Hengler's Magic Circus. The fact that knives were used in the Phoenix Park Murders points, according to the logic of the small-minded cabmen, to the fact that foreigners must have been hired to do the killing: a knife, by custom, is not an Irish weapon. The tattoo that adorns Murphy itself is chimerical: if one pulls the skin, the young man's face changes. Significantly, the tattoo includes the number of this episode—sixteen; and, to some critics, this number signifies homosexuality, though this surmise, of course, is only that, a surmise; yet it is interesting that the number "16" is associated in Europe with homosexuality, just as "69" is associated in the United States with homosexuality.

Returning to the idea of dissipation and tiredness, the patrons of Fitzharris's establishment are willing to argue so long as no blows are exchanged, a trite and tired (and Irish) standard. They resemble the peasants in Synge's *Playboy of the Western World*; these people admire

Christy Mahon's blather about killing his father until the father reappears in person; then Christy, apparently, truly must kill the man. Again, the facts about Skin-the-Goat are wrong; he did not drive the car used by the murderers; he drove only the *decoy* car. And the newspaper report of Dignam's funeral is thoroughly phony in both its praise of the deceased and also in its factual information.

Finally, in "Eumaeus," poor Bloom reveals only too clearly his desperate need to be accepted – as well as to accept – that is, he needs to be comforted, as well as to comfort. The usually equanimous Bloom is still brooding over the insult by the Citizen in "The Cyclops" and, to make his point, pitiably he denies his Jewishness on a technicality: "though in reality I'm not." Later, he again (sycophantically) turns the conversation around to Molly, showing an outdated photo to an indifferent Stephen. And his plans for "shanghai-ing" Stephen into a singing career are countered by the three turds dropped by a horse at the close of the episode.

The Dublin that Joyce presents in "Eumaeus" is a particularly distressing one, resembling Conrad's description of London in *The Secret Agent*: an aquarium after the water has been drained.

Chapter 17:   Ithaca

"Ithaca" takes place at Bloom's house at 7 Eccles St. at about 2:00 A.M. on June 17. Bloom and Stephen discuss a huge variety of topics; Bloom makes Stephen cocoa (Joyce implies that this is a "communion"), and, after Stephen leaves, Bloom assesses his day's activities and gingerly crawls into bed beside Molly in an upside-down position, kissing her rump. The sleepy Molly asks him what he has been doing all day (and night), and Bloom supplies a partial litany of the events, leaving out anything incriminating.

The contrast of Bloom's actions with those of Odysseus is crucial. Odysseus and Telemachus united at the end of the *Odyssey* in order to kill the suitors who had insisted on courting Penelope until she chose among them. Bloom, the passive twentieth-century anti-hero treats Molly's infidelity with the "suitor" Boylan with acceptance and generosity. Although he reserves the right to divorce Molly at a later date and although he considers using witnesses to catch her in some future act, these thoughts of his are only a small part of the emotional complexity with which he approaches his sad situation. Here, Bloom experiences envy, jealousy, abnegation, and equanimity, but Joyce makes it clear that Bloom's feelings consist mainly of "more abnegation than jealousy, less envy than equanimity." Bloom, as a modern humanist, sees Molly's affair as part of the natural pattern of the universe: what happened was due to woman's instincts and the impulsiveness of Boylan's youth. Besides, although Boylan thinks that he is unique, he is "the last term of a preceding series. . . ." This "series," however, is not to be taken literally; instead, Joyce means for us to understand it as part of a vast cosmic theme – that is, the list of lovers which Bloom supplies for us is a product of his *fancy*, an attempt by him to assuage the pain of his present feeling of separateness from Molly.

The style of "Ithaca," with its question-and-answer format and its "scientized" language, has caused critics some difficulty. Joyce, while admitting that the format of "Ithaca" is indeed difficult, called the chapter his own personal favorite. And the style does fulfill several functions. Its catechetical nature supplies a religious basis for the discussion between Bloom and Stephen. And, if the chapter can be said to have a true narrator, he is a vast Olympian figure who can place seemingly important but really ephemeral mortals and their actions into the perspective of a large cosmic consciousness. In fact, "Ithaca" is Joyce's preparation (his preliminary groundwork) for *Finnegans Wake*, with its shadowy, hulking archetypal personages. Finally, the "objectivity" of the episode permits Bloom to use the screen of logic as a kind of filter in order to bear the almost unendurable pain which he feels from Molly's assignation. He perceived Boylan's presence almost from the start of the chapter – as early as the incident of the betting tickets that Boylan tore up in anger after Sceptre lost the race. What is perhaps most regrettable about the assignation itself is that Molly and Blazes make no real attempt to disguise the adultery. Bloom, however, imagines the act; he, in a sense, uses fancy and imagination to disguise the painful blatancy of the adultery; now he is confronted with its direct evidence – that is, with the facts of its physical reality: for example, there are the chairs, rearranged so that the two lovers could sit beside each other to sing "Love's Old Sweet Song"; there are also the cigarette butts, as well as a male's impression in the Blooms' bed, and also there are the traces of Plumtree's Potted Meat (Boylan, metaphorically, "potted" Molly with his "meat").

The concept of marital infidelity bothered Joyce himself greatly throughout his relationship with his wife, Nora. Joyce's play, *Exiles*, hinges upon Richard Rowan's fear that Bertha has been unfaithful, and here, in *Ulysses*, in the "Scylla and Charybdis" chapter, Shakespeare is seen to have suffered throughout his life from the thought of a loved one who had betrayed him. "Ithaca" must have been extremely difficult for Joyce to write; for this reason, it is reasonable to conclude that he handled his wound of doubt by putting an aesthetic distance between Bloom-Joyce and the corrupted Molly. Significantly, in "Penelope," Joyce has Molly think of Bloom at the very end of her soliloquy and respond with a resounding "Yes."

Joyce was able, through literature, to sublimate his psychic wound into a brilliant episode that securely places man's pedestrian maneuverings among the stars. Bloom's entrance into 7 Eccles St. sees him "move freely in space," as he jumps two feet and ten inches (a fact that he later thinks is acrobatic). Joyce's description of water (while Bloom is in the kitchen with Stephen) is not merely a tour de force, but it is an attempt by Joyce to again use one of his "catalogues" to compress, as it were, all the world into *Ulysses*. Bloom's and Stephen's common perception of the "incertitude of the void" is communicated by an intuitive (though transient) *oneness* that they share during a few moments in this chapter, and as Joyce says, the oneness is: "Not verbally. [but] Substantially." And the vision that occurs just before Stephen's departure, his Ascension into Heaven, is the "heaventree of stars"; it parallels Bloom's own Ascent at the end of "The Cyclops." After Stephen leaves, Bloom, now alone, feels the "cold of interstellar space. . . ." Here, his perception matches that of Gabriel Conroy in a story from *Dubliners*, "The Dead," when Gabriel learns that when his wife, Gretta, was very young, she was in love with a young man who died for her; in the short story, snow covers all of Ireland, and it becomes another symbol of universality. It may be that it is this terrible chill which Bloom feels, this prescience of death, that leads him to return to his wife's bed, to the Womb of the great Earth Mother Gea-Tellus, and to resume the position of a half-comic, half-pathetic, but in some ways heroic, reverse Buddha.

Another dimension is added to the Ithaca Eisode's catechetical structure by the vast amount of religious imagery which Joyce uses in the episode, even though the references do not form a strict pattern. On one level, the religious symbolism takes the form of numbers; particularly, the 3's and 9's found in the chapter are ultimately suggestive of the Trinity; in addition, Bloom's first poem, written when he was eleven years old (the age which Rudy would be on December 29, had he lived), was composed in response to the *Shamrock*'s offering of "*three* [emphasis added] prizes"; and here, one recalls St. Patrick's apocryphal demonstration of the feasibility of the Trinity by illustrating its three-in-one nature with a shamrock. Also, in *Ulysses*, Bloom and Stephen are loosely coalescing together for the *third* time in their lives. Also, Bloom was baptized three times, the third time in the same church and by the same priest as Stephen; and in this arithmetical chapter, the 3's (as noted) are often transmuted into 9's. Reinforcing this religious number symbolism is Joyce's use of many terms that can be read on a literal, as well as on a theological, level: crosslaid sticks, lucifer matches, host, mass, and so forth.

Sometimes in "Ithaca," however, the religious imagery is not simply flecked over the pages; instead, it is used to expand upon the larger issues of *Ulysses*. The ceremony, for example, with which Bloom leads Stephen into his home with a candle after taking off his hat suggests both the beginning of Mass, in which the priest removes his biretta, and it also suggests the entrance of the catechumen (this time, Stephen) into the catacombs, where the novice convert will be asked several questions to determine the strength of his belief. Stephen's departure ends one "Mass" of *Ulysses*, and his ashplant becomes the crucifix carried from the church at the end of a religious ceremony; the bells in the church of Saint George ring to signal its conclusion. In the theological context of the chapter, the bee sting suffered by Bloom becomes the spear which pierced Christ's side, and his sore "footsoles" (a play on the word "soul") suggest the feet of Christ, which were pierced by nails.

It is fashionable today to view this religious symbolism in "Ithaca" as being suggestive of a Tri-union of Bloom, Stephen, and Molly, in which Bloom and Stephen share elements of God the Father and God the Son and in which Molly becomes the Mystical Bride – that is, the Bride of the Catholic Church. It is more probable, however, that Joyce is using religion as a metaphor to suggest the elevated possibilities that human nature can reach in certain moments. In contrast, at times, the intellectuality of Stephen and the crass materialism of Bloom fuse in a mystical, unspoken way. But *Ulysses*, one must always keep in mind, is basically a comic novel; it is *not* a theological treatise. At the zenith of their aspirations, Bloom and Stephen urinate alongside one another, with the urine becoming the modern, symbolic equivalent of sacramental wine. And, of course, the pedestrian Bloom will always dream of a bourgeois country estate and wonder how human excrement can be used industrially.

Chapter 18: Penelope

In Homer's epic, Odysseus is reunited with Penelope after he has slain the numerous suitors. At first, however, Penelope does not recognize her husband; she is convinced that he is indeed Odysseus, her husband, only after he is able to describe to her the construction of their bed, a fact known only to the two of them. In Joyce, the scene for "Penelope" is the Blooms' bed, whose jingling sound has been heard, vocally foreshadowed, and developed through several motifs in *Ulysses* throughout this single day of June 16th, 1904.

Joyce's technique in "Penelope" is illustrated not so much by stream-of-consciousness narrative as it is developed by word association—that is, Molly's thoughts do not "flow" in a consecutive, narrative pattern; instead, in "Penelope," Joyce reproduces the seemingly random ideas of a sleepy woman in the wee hours of the morning. This technique suggests that Molly is infinity, whose symbol is a horizontal 8. Molly (Marion Tweedy) was born on September 8, 1870, and on her birthday, Molly recalls, Bloom once bought her eight poppies. Recumbent as she is in this episode, Molly's physical position suggests mathematical infinity—the "infinite variety" of womanhood. Countering this amorphous non-structure is Joyce's use of only *eight* sentences to compose and impose some measure of order on the episode. Also, "Penelope" both begins and ends with Molly's thoughts about Bloom. Beyond this, however, little can be said about any more stringent pattern. Joyce has said that "Penelope" revolves around "four cardinal points . . . the female breasts, arse, womb and. . . ." Later, however, he contradicted himself, implying that in "Penelope," he was trying to portray the untamed torrent of womanhood.

It seems more profitable, ultimately, to examine the character of Molly herself, for she is one of the most intriguing characters in all of fiction. She resembles, first of all, Chaucer's Wife of Bath. The key to Molly's character is perhaps best contained in her statement, her cry, really, to: "let us have a bit of fun. . . ." Also, as with the Wife of

Bath, a current of melancholy runs through Molly's personality. She doesn't want to be *used* by Boylan; she wants to be loved, in a *tender* way. Molly wishes that some man, any man, would give her a long kiss while holding her *lovingly* in his arms. Molly Bloom is lonely, and she writes letters to herself; she has been rejected by her quirkish and often cold husband, who also writes letters to a chimera figure (Martha Clifford). But, basically, Molly is not a defeated woman – despite her disappointments in finding a man who is able to love her; like Chaucer's heroine, Molly is a survivor, and Molly knows *all* the feminine tricks. Today, for example, Molly's technique of wooing might be similar to "faking an orgasm": "I gave my eyes that look with my hair a bit loose from the tumbling. . . ." And her method of lovemaking has always been mingled with a touch of teasing fantasy. When she was very young, Molly told Lieutenant Mulvey that she was engaged to a Spanish nobleman, Don Miguel de la Flora – and, as it turned out, she did *indeed* marry a "flower," in the figure of Bloom (his pseudonym), and he is another person who fantasizes about his love life with his pen pal, Martha.

Another intriguing and major trait of Molly Bloom is her jealousy, her scorn of other women. She criticizes Mrs. Riordan (Stephen's tutor in *A Portrait*) for leaving money to have prayers said for the repose of her soul, instead of making a small bequest to the Blooms, who had befriended her. In addition, Molly fired the Blooms' maid, Mary Driscoll, on a fictitious charge of stealing oysters – simply because Bloom had taken a fancy to the girl. And Molly is still jealous of Bloom's old flame, Josie Powell, whom she thinks Bloom may have met at Dignam's funeral, and she makes up reasons for her feeling fortunate to have Bloom as a husband instead of her being married to the lunatic Denis Breen, whom Josie married. She has heard that Breen goes to bed in muddy boots, and she knows that he is now the laughing stock of Dublin. In addition, Molly resents her competitor, the singer Kathleen Kearney (who appears in the short story "A Mother" in *Dubliners*). Molly also takes pride in the fact that when she was a girl her hair was thicker than Hester's, her girl friend's, (and thus she reminds one of Hedda Gabler, who wanted to burn off her rival's hair in Ibsen's play). In addition, when Molly reminisces through the mists of years about her young lover, Mulvey, who she thinks is probably around forty by now (1904), she imagines that he is married and takes pride in the fact that *she* had him first (masturbating him into a handkerchief).

Molly is refreshing, even when her scornful criticism is directed towards Joyce's other characters in the novel, for her observations shed new insights into their actions and motivations. For example, Molly assails the "boiled eyes" of Menton, the pompous lawyer. She wonders if Paul de Kock, the author of salacious novels, was so nicknamed because he was "going about with his tube from one woman to another. . . ." and she sees Simon Dedalus as both flirtatious and overly critical.

Likewise, Molly's skepticism is directed with special vigor towards the two men in her life, Boylan and Bloom. Boylan slapped Molly on the rump a bit too familiarly as he was leaving; afterward, she feels, and quite rightly, that she is *not* a horse *or* an ass. Neither did he show much manliness when, at her insistence, he withdrew from her in order to prevent pregnancy (the final time, though, he did complete the act). Nor is Boylan very sophisticated: he undressed in front of her so matter-of-factly that Molly was annoyed. Perhaps, she wonders, he was simply taking her for granted. Even while dreaming of becoming Mrs. Boylan, Molly knows that this union will never come about, and she wonders musingly how she can extort presents from her lover.

But it is Molly's portrait of Bloom that is most crucial to an understanding of *Ulysses*, for in her thoughts about Bloom, we can see that Molly's adultery was triggered, basically, by the failings of two people. We sympathized with Bloom throughout the novel; now, in "Penelope," we hear Molly's side of the story.

Bloom is quirkish in many ways — apart from his sexual abnormalities. Although Bloom can be pleasant to beggars and waiters, he is often irascible with others, especially employers, and Molly wonders when he will lose his present job because of his know-it-all ways. Bloom's glib commonplace that Christ was the first Socialist made the sensitive Molly cry. And Molly is aware that while Bloom pretends indifference to pretty girls, he is often ogling them with a sly eye. Bloom really does *not* like to work (despite all of his moralizing to Stephen in "Eumaeus"); instead, he would rather stay around the house all day, getting under Molly's feet. Bloom is a bit of a faker; once he pretended to know how to row, and he almost drowned himself and Molly. Another time, he thought that he heard a burglar, and he came down the steps trembling, making enough noise to scare off any possible thief. Additionally, Molly can't stand Bloom's way of sleeping: if he jerks his feet, she might lose her teeth; and how can she even break wind with him at the *foot* of the bed? Bloom is so parsimonious and suspicious that he locks his checkbook away, and Molly has been tempted, on the few occasions when he left the dresser drawer open, to forge his name on a number of checks and cash them.

But it is Bloom's sexual habits that have, most of all, alienated Molly, as they would most people. Once, Bloom asked Molly to walk in horse dung, revealing his revolting perversion for coprophilia. He also begged her once to give him a snippet of her underwear. He has written her dirty letters, and Bloom once proposed that he take naked pictures of her to sell. After the birth of Milly, Bloom asked, since Molly's breasts were still expanded, that he milk her into the tea. Molly feels that the cold feet that Bloom lays on her in bed reflect his cold heart. Molly has truly become over the years a victim of the "loveless Irish marriage," pointed out by Synge, among others, in his *In the Shadow of the Glen*. Molly, to some extent, resents Bloom's bringing Stephen home (although she fantasizes about Stephen's future existence in the Blooms' house): perhaps Bloom wants Stephen to make love to her, a point cited by some critics who have detected a hint of homosexuality in Bloom's sometimes obsessive relationship with Stephen.

It is Molly's own sexuality, however, that has inspired so much critical acclaim and so much denunciation. Some critics think of Molly as a "pig"; others see her as Joyce's symbol of the Blessed Mother, finding an aura of sacramentality in her combining menstrual blood and water (urine) in a cracked chamber pot. The truth is probably somewhere in between these two extremes: Molly is religious, insofar as she accepts God and His manifestations in physical nature. She is also completely human in her total acceptance of the body, with all of its joys and pains. Through Molly, Joyce revealed what Irish women were really thinking when their subconscious gates were flung open on a warm June night in 1904.

Many of Molly's thoughts touch on subjects simply not discussed in the literature of 1922 – at least not outside of a psychoanalyst's office – and Joyce reveals great insight into the physical aspects of the female personality. The variety of sexual experiences that Molly touches upon is astounding: the kinky habits of Mrs. Mastiansky's husband, for example, who made his wife "stick out her tongue as far as ever she could. . . ." There is also flagellation, as well as exhibitionists who pretend that they are urinating in order to expose themselves; in addition, there is female masturbation (complete with banana); a wish to exchange places with a man to see how sex feels from the male viewpoint; a desire to make love to boys and sailors, even though the latter might be diseased; and a stray thought of having sex with Boylan in front of Bloom in order to punish him – these thoughts, plus many more, crowd her mind and flow from it.

What "Penelope" concerns most, however, is Molly's frank acceptance of herself, and most of what Molly thinks about is scarcely "abnormal" by late twentieth-century standards: for example, the shape, in detail, of the male sex organ; Boylan's stallion-like sexual prowess (it seems that he had at least four climaxes); a woman's vaginal irritation before a period; rough sex hastening a period; and the physical enjoyment of using a chamber pot (note Bloom's delight in defecation).

With all of Molly's untutored insights into the human condition, her full acceptance of the fun of life, one question remains for the reader of *Ulysses*: what is to be the future relationship between Molly and Bloom? Although the question is ultimately unanswerable (for anyone), Joyce does provide several clues or workpoints that argue to a possible reconciliation. The breakfast in bed that Molly will probably cook for Bloom later in the morning of June 17 and her memory of the encounter on Howth Hill, when she led Bloom into proposing to her, are the bookends of this chapter. Both of them contain symbols of rebirth: if the breakfast is to be cooked, it will consist of eggs, usually a symbol of rebirth in Joyce; and Molly's thoughts of the younger, more handsome Bloom include the moment when she passed into his mouth "the bit of seedcake," another hint of rebirth.

The real "evidence" of a future for the Blooms, however, is to be found in how well she knows him. As was noted earlier, Molly is on to all of his tricks. She knows of his pornographic collecting, of his eating habits when he has a crush on a new woman, of his blotting out a letter (to Martha), of his particular susceptibility to maneuvering females (since he is almost forty), of his avoiding the house when he is guiltily in love, and of the fact that other people make fun of him behind his back. Yet she is still able to remember what he was like, and her ending memories present a much better and less farcical Bloom than we have seen throughout the rest of *Ulysses*.

And is it possible for a timid advertising salesman ever to break up with someone who knows his faults so well – and who accepts them in her own peculiar way?

CHARACTER ANALYSES

Leopold Bloom

The first impression that one has of Leopold Bloom, Joyce's modern equivalent of Ulysses and also Joyce's Wandering Jew, is that Bloom is as much of an outsider in Dublin as his prototypes were in their peregrinations through various foreign countries. Bloom is shut off from his Roman Catholic, often anti-Semitic associates, first of all, because of religious differences. Stephen's discussion with the anti-Semite Deasy in "Nestor" foreshadows the treatment that Bloom is to receive throughout the day. In "Hades," Bloom is patronized by the three other occupants of the carriage that is headed towards Glasnevin Cemetery, and, in that episode, his conciliatory views of suicide stun the conservative Catholic Dubliners. In "Scylla and Charybdis," Mulligan detects hints of (besides repressed homosexuality) the Jew in Bloom's physiognomy, and he warns Stephen away from him. In "The Cyclops," Bloom, before fighting back, is degraded by the rabidly anti-Semitic Citizen.

There are many other indications of Bloom's alienation – from home and from community – in the novel. He is a "keyless" hero (as is Stephen), having left the key to 7 Eccles St. in his other trousers and having been afraid to retrieve it because he might disturb Molly. His name is mutilated into "L. Boom" in the newspaper report of Dignam's funeral. There is no room for him in the *Freeman's* offices in "Aeolus," and he is struck at one point, although accidentally, by an opening door. Even his "greasy eyes," which Lydia Douce, a barmaid at the Ormond Hotel, notices as Bloom passes by with *Sweets of Sin* under his arm, are enough to establish him as a figure of ridicule.

Thus there is a good deal of pathos in Bloom's portrayal. Thinking of his own father's suicide while others condemn the act on the way to Glasnevin Cemetery, Bloom states, "They used to drive a stake of wood through his [the suicide's] heart in the grave. As if it wasn't broken already." Again, Bloom thinks constantly during this day, June 16, of Boylan's and Molly's adultery, yet he still manages to get through his wretched day – and to perform several charitable acts: "Today. Today. Not think." One must feel sympathy for Bloom when he sits in the Ormond Hotel, cut off from the convivial group's enjoyment of Ben Dollard's rendition of "The Croppy Boy," whose lyrics remind Bloom so much of his own dead son, Rudy: "I alone am left of my name and race."

Bloom does bring some of his troubles upon himself, however, and in *Ulysses*, Joyce clearly does not present a plaster saint as protagonist. Bloom seems unable to speak in plain language, at least around Molly, and she is vexed by his definition of "metempsychosis" as the "transmigration of souls." Again, Bloom has the fatalistic habit of accepting many things that perhaps should not be accepted, of closing his eyes, for example, to the fact of Boylan's letter to Molly which protrudes from under her pillow, and to his daughter's possible loss of her virginity in the near future. Also, Bloom does not seem to want any result to issue from his correspondence with Martha Clifford; perhaps he would rather stand on a beach and masturbate, as he does in "Nausicaa," an act that does not demand commitment. As noted, Bloom does a number of things to antagonize those around him, who are already only too willing to condemn him: he puts nothing in black and white; he never buys drinks; as "Mister Knowall," he expounds at great length on the reasons that a hanged man undergoes a sexual erection at the time of death, adding to the already tense atmosphere of Barney Kiernan's pub in "The Cyclops," and although he helps Stephen in the later episodes of *Ulysses*, he is not averse to considering how Stephen can further his plans for a touring musical company.

Despite his faults, however, Bloom does perform such a remarkable number of charitable deeds in the novel that he becomes, in many ways, a modern Christ. He attends Dignam's funeral, for example, despite his knowing that he will not be accepted by the other mourners, and, later, he visits Paddy's widow to help her understand the life insurance policy. (Ironically, he met Cunningham in Kiernan's pub for that purpose and was accused of being a defrauder of widows and children.) Bloom feeds Banbury cakes to hungry sea gulls. He pities the starving Dedalus children. He helps a blind youth cross a street. He goes to Dr. Horne's hospital to look in upon Mina Purefoy, who has lain three days in labor, and he stays after the birth to watch over Stephen, who he thinks is being covertly made drunk by Mulligan. In Nighttown, Bloom cares for Stephen, even though he must run to catch up with him; he saves Stephen's money from the scheming Bella Cohen; he tries to persuade a soldier not to strike the incapable Stephen; and when Stephen is knocked down, Bloom takes him home, first stopping at a cabman's shelter to find some sustenance for him.

But in deciding whether or not Bloom is, finally, a "saint" or "sinner," one must realize that *Ulysses* is basically a *comic* novel and that Bloom is a very humorous figure. He thinks nothing of slipping his kidney from Dlugacz's into his pocket. He surreptitiously walks in a circle to pick up his letter from Martha Clifford (and is frustrated when M'Coy's chatter forestalls his reading it). He tries to follow the Woods' maid out of Dlugacz's but cannot do so. In Glasnevin Cemetery, his misreading of the Catholic ritual is as humorous as the discussion of suicide on the way to the cemetery was painful. And all of his efforts at concealment, Bloom was detected in the museum staring at the creases between the buttocks of the statues of nude women.

Joyce's portrait of Bloom, then, is one of a thoroughly whole man, one who can enjoy defecating, urinating, eating fried kidneys, and contemplating water; one whose sexual perversities, fully explored in "Circe" and in "Penelope," are balanced against the magnanimities of his personality. Indeed, in Bloom, Joyce has portrayed God's plenty, a sometimes pedestrian man, but a person for whom the physical world does emphatically exist.

Stephen Dedalus

In *A Portrait of the Artist as a Young Man*, Stephen was treated with both irony and sympathy. Joyce admired his young protagonist's battle against orthodoxy, but he also found Stephen's intolerant cynicism a bit pompous. In Book Five of *A Portrait*, Stephen became a mock Christ figure, preaching his gospel of aesthetics to bored and sometimes gibing apostles. In *Ulysses*, Stephen is a more human figure than he appeared to be at the end of the earlier novel. He has returned from Paris, his destination at the end of *A Portrait*, having been summoned home by word of his mother's incipient death from cancer; now he finds himself emotionally drowning as surely as his mother literally drowned in her own green bile. In *Ulysses*, he sees himself as an Icarus-like figure, one who flew too high and burned his wings in the sun; as "Daedalus," he parallels himself with the archetypal flying ace.

In *Ulysses*, Stephen is beset with many problems, some of them stemming from his emotional distance from those around him, whom he cannot accept. Although he lives in the Martello Tower with Haines, the Oxonian, and with Buck Mulligan, a Dublin medical student, he knows that he cannot remain in this habitat: Haines has bizarre nightmares that keep Stephen awake, and Mulligan, with his coarse and brutal treatment of Stephen, has "usurped" Stephen's place in the Tower. At the end of "Telemachus," he meekly surrenders the Tower's key to Mulligan and begins to walk his own path. Compared to the physical Mulligan, Stephen feels himself to be inept and weak. Stephen is afraid of water (symbolically, baptism), while Mulligan plunges into life. In many ways, Stephen is physically withdrawn, fearing dogs and thunder, while Mulligan once saved a man from drowning. The facile Mulligan can handle the visiting milk woman in "Telemachus," although he looks down upon her, while Stephen sits brooding upon the lost past of Ireland. Stephen's estrangement is also seen in his teaching at Mr. Deasy's school, where he does not seem to care, really, that his students are inattentive and obstreperous.

Stephen's sense of abstraction, of distance, forces him to turn inward for answers, and, it is through Stephen's vexed psyche and soul that Joyce presents, especially in "Proteus," that we see his young man's bewilderment over the changing, "protean," nature of reality. Divested of his former stringent religious beliefs, wishing to become a famous writer though sometimes doubting his ability to do so, Stephen, in "Proteus," is searching for his origins. He imagines that the two old women that he sees on the beach are midwives; he projects an image of navel cords linking all humanity and ending with Eve, "belly without blemish." He wonders who his real father is: Simon, whose part in Stephen's conception was physiological; or God Himself, Who may have planned the event from all eternity.

Stephen's ruminations lead him to feel a great sense of guilt, which is augmented by his tender conscience, one that focuses upon blemishes and ignores virtues. Stephen feels guilty for many things: he refused to pray at his dying mother's bedside; he smokes Haines's tobacco, yet he treats him with disdain; he borrowed a pound from the theosophist George Russell (A. E.) and spent it on a prostitute; as the eldest Dedalus child, he abandoned his starving sisters to a poverty which was worsened by an alcoholic father who spends his time in bars while the family barely survives; he led a false existence when he was a youth, pretending so well that he was deeply pious that he was singled out for training in the priesthood, yet all the time, he was thinking of naked women.

Thus Stephen's portrait wins a great deal of sympathy from the reader. With eyeglasses that were broken on June 15, Stephen sees physical reality and the outer movements of life through a myopic opacity. His salary from Mr. Deasy is meager, and the tiresome headmaster uses his young instructor as a sounding board for his trite ideas. Stephen's concept of Shakespeare is treated with scorn in "Scylla and Charybdis," and he is not invited to the literary get-together to be held at the house of the writer George Moore on the evening of Bloomsday. He is patronized by George Russell (A. E.), who only reluctantly agrees to print Mr. Deasy's letter about foot and mouth disease (which Deasy had given Stephen) in his farmers' magazine. Stephen stumbles through Nighttown in an alcoholic daze, caused in part by his friends' giving him the disguised drinks; then, he meets his mother in a horrifying hallucination, is abandoned by his friend Lynch, and, when helpless, he is knocked down by the British soldier Carr. Even Bloom, despite all of his sympathy for Stephen, who he feels is wasting his talents among drifters and prostitutes, "uses" Stephen; Bloom thinks that perhaps Stephen can abet Bloom's imaginary concert tours—or teach Italian to Molly.

Yet, despite the pathos of his situation (which Joyce "controls" by undercutting it with many acerbic statements by Stephen), the ultimate picture of Stephen in *Ulysses* is heroic. Mulligan may be the sure *doer*, but Stephen is the sensitive *thinker*: Stephen dwells upon the implications of sin; Buck hides any possible guilt beneath blasphemies. Stephen did indeed suffer because of his mother's death: he "wept alone." Stephen is the complex Prince Hamlet; Mulligan is more a Rosencrantz than a true Horatio. Stephen, throughout *Ulysses*, is courageously pursuing the goal which he set for himself in *A Portrait*: to break free of society's nets—that is, to break free from all the forces which inhibit the growth of the soul and, by implication, the growth of the artist. For example, he refuses to join the national movement which was developing in Ireland in 1904: political aspirations, as Stephen knows from the fall of Charles Stewart Parnell, lead only to dismal failure. Stephen feels that the Irish Renaissance is simply insular – a cultural suicide, through which Ireland will cut itself off from the wellsprings of European thought. Despite all of their posturings, Irishmen, to Stephen, are still bound to the double tyrants of Britain and Rome.

Stephen is going through a difficult period in *Ulysses* – but Joyce's tone is optimistic. We feel when we end the novel that Stephen will probably find solutions to his problems.

Molly Bloom

The Penelope Episode of *Ulysses* presents a full picture of Molly Bloom, one told through her own sleepy thoughts. In "Penelope," Molly emerges as a thoroughly real person: freely accepting her sexual self, jealous of other women, sometimes melancholic, demanding when dealing with a lover, and completely knowledge-able about her husband's eccentricities.

Yet Molly is also a symbolic figure, and her characterzation in the entire novel contains several tiers of meaning. Molly is, first of all, an embodiment of archetypal womanhood. She reminds the reader of the Pagan Mary whom Stephen saw standing in the water at the close of Book Four of *A Portrait of the Artist as a Young Man*. At that point, Stephen resisted the temptation offered by a fully sensual but limiting person – that is, someone who might comfort him with her flesh but divert him from pursuing the more intellec-tual goal of becoming an independent writer. In *A Portrait*, Stephen's "dream girl" had traits of a mermaid, as a trail of seaweed fastened itself upon her body. Molly, too, is both a mermaid and in "Calypso," she is a symbol of the enchantress who kept Odysseus away from Ithaca for several years. Molly's retort to Bloom's defini-tion of "metempsychosis": "O, rocks!" establishes her as a siren (Molly is of course a concert singer) whose song may well lead mariners to deadly shoals. Also typifying her universal womanhood is her menstruation, which links her with Milly Bloom and Martha Clifford. Again, Molly's image as woman-temptress is seen in the role of Kitty O'Shea, who was instrumental in causing Parnell's downfall: like Molly, the wife of Captain O'Shea was a "fine lump of a woman"; and, as did Parnell, Bloom is now struggling to establish Home Rule, not so much political independence for Ireland as sovereignty for himself at 7 Eccles St. Finally, Molly has all the elements of the Blooms' mysterious, enigmatic cat, who warmly stretches itself in the Blooms' house and is reluctant (as Molly seems to be) to leave the building. When Bloom wonders why mice don't scream when being devoured by cats, he may well be thinking of his own situation.

Although Molly is Joyce's equivalent of an earth goddess, one for whose warm flesh Bloom longs, she is an aging and very hefty beauty who has a "reputation" (deserved or not) in Dublin. Jack Power's ambiguous query about "*Madame*" in the carriage on the way to Glasnevin Cemetery paints her as a symbolic whore mistress, though that is not, of course, Power's intention. Lenehan feels free to tell M'Coy (in the ninth section of "The Wandering Rocks") of taking liberties with Molly, describing her "milky way," during an evening in 1894 while Bloom was pointing out the stars as the group returned from the "big spread out at Glencree reformatory. . . ." (Apparently, ten years later, Molly still has her "name.") Molly is a topic of conversation in "The Cyclops" as the acid-tongued narrator, the Nameless One, the Citizen, says of Bloom, "The fat heap he married is a nice old phenomenon with a back on her like a ballalley." And the picture of Molly that Bloom shows an indifferent Stephen in "Eumaeus" is outdated: in the cabman's shelter, Bloom is desperately trying to recapture a vision of Molly as she once was.

Molly is an earth goddess, then, but a fading one; she is also a Calypso who is herself held captive in a loveless marriage. Her lover, Boylan, is crass and insensitive, and her husband, uxorious, almost masochistic. Bloom makes her breakfast exactly as she demands, sends Milly away to facilitate the Blazes-Molly affair, relinquishes his key to the house (and to the marriage) through his fear of awakening her, brings her Boylan's letter of assignation, orders skin lotion for her and is desperate when he forgets to return to Sweny's to pick it up, rents the pornographic *Sweets of Sin* for her, and he ends the day by kissing her rump. It is no wonder that Molly's sexual fantasies sometimes contain hints of her own masochism; for example, one of her favorite books is *Ruby: The Pride of the Ring*, which is about a naked woman who is seduced by a sadistic male. And adding to the pathos of Molly's situation is Bloom's inability to tell her how he really feels about her. In "The Sirens," the reader knows that Bloom has chosen Molly over the platonic Martha, and it is unfortunate that Molly does not know of his decision.

Joyce suggests in *Ulysses*, however, that all the marital pain experienced by Molly and Bloom *may* eventually be turned into joy of a sort. By the end of her soliloquy in "Penelope," Molly has all but written off Boylan as a possible future husband. Also, she will probably accede to Bloom's demand for breakfast in bed – and her last thoughts are of him. One must not forget the Bloomsday date of *Ulysses*, almost certainly the day on which Joyce himself knew that he was in love with Nora Barnacle. Preoccupied as he was with the concept of marital infidelity, perhaps Joyce placed the affair of Blazes and Molly on this date to suggest a gleam of hope for the future. Having seen through Boylan's facade, perhaps Molly will once again unite meaningfully with Bloom.

Hugh "Blazes" Boylan

Molly Bloom presents the most complete picture of her lover of June 16, 1904 in "Penelope," but other glimpses of Blazes Boylan are scattered throughout *Ulysses*. In fact, Boylan's presence in Bloom's mind is ubiquitous, and several times in the novel, Bloom's thoughts of his rival call forth his physical appearance. Bloom's daughter, Milly, has been sent to Mulligar by her father so that she will be away from home during the upcoming affair; yet her letter mentions Boylan: "Tell him silly Milly sends my best respects." On the way to Glasnevin Cemetery (in "Hades"), Boylan passes by the carriage of mourners; and Simon Dedalus, Martin Cunningham, and Jack Power all praise Boylan – as Bloom sits quietly staring at his nails (a Christocentric symbol since Bloom is being nailed to the Cross by the marital infidelity), and he wonders how otherwise sensible men can like the "worst man in Dublin." In "The Lestrygonians," Bloom's thoughts that Boylan may have venereal disease (an improbable, passing, though painful consideration) precede Boylan's appearance, and the sight of his trademarks, a straw hat and tan shoes, forces Bloom to flee into the museum. When Bloom does manage to summon the courage to follow Boylan into the Ormond Hotel in "The Sirens," he sits in another room so that Boylan can't see him, as Boylan "warms up" with a drink before his meeting with Molly.

Despite the fact that Boylan is a "man's man"—a manager of a fighter, an advertising man, and a fine singer in a city that venerated the male voice—Joyce makes it clear that Blazes is a shallow sort, in many ways a stereotypical seducer. When Blazes stops into Thornton's to purchase a bottle of wine and some fruit to be sent to Molly before his visit, he looks down into the salesgirl's blouse, and Joyce permits the reader a glance at Boylan's thought processes: he regards the young woman simply as a "young pullet," and he thus reveals his inability to see beyond the physical. Molly has so little trust in the tricky Boylan (he once spread rumors that his fighter was drinking beer during training and then made money by betting on his underdog) that she thinks the presents might be Boylan's way of avoiding the assignation.

In many ways, then, Boylan is a humorous self-parody, a Dublin Priapus. He flirts with the (not unwilling) bargirls in the Ormond Hotel just before he leaves to see Molly, and the expression associated with him, "Cockcarracarra," signals both his sexual capacities and his conscienceless betrayal of human emotions. And Joyce suggests that, even after experiencing (possibly) four sexual climaxes with Molly, Boylan *may* be the man who, having lost on the Gold Cup Race, has come to Nighttown in "Circe" to find a prostitute.

Nor does Boylan make any attempt to cover up his deeds, even though he does know Bloom personally. In "Ithaca," Bloom finds several obvious signs of Boylan's recent presence: torn-up betting tickets, a depleted bottle of port, furniture rearranged so that Boylan and Molly could sing "Love's Old Sweet Song" together, cigarette butts, and an impression left in the Blooms' bed by a male (not Bloom). The crumbs of Plumtree's Potted Meat, carelessly left in this Penelopian bed, suggest the vulgarity of Boylan's lovemaking, since "to pot the meat" is Dublin slang for sexual intercourse.

Nor does Boylan deceive Molly, who is only too aware of his vulgarity. Boylan undressed casually in front of her, slapped her on the rump in a too familiar manner as he was leaving, and probably allowed Molly to determine the tone and manner of their sex. Molly does not deceive herself into believing that she and Boylan have any chance of a future together; she is using Boylan for relief from a quirkish husband as much as he is using her, and she considers how she can force him to buy presents for her. Molly knows how jealous and angry Boylan can be, however, and she hopes that Bloom does not change his mind and decide to accompany the two on the upcoming concert tour. She would have to sleep with Bloom in one room, and Boylan would be in another, and he would never believe that nothing sexual occurred between her and Bloom. Then too, Boylan did tear up the losing racing tickets right in front of her in a fit of anger, not a very sophisticated way to act on a first seduction.

Given Boylan's coarseness, it is possible that Bloom may win Molly back, after all. Boylan's phallic choice in the Gold Cup, Sceptre, did lose the race, which was won by the darkhorse, Throwaway, symbolic of Bloom. Molly will probably accede to Bloom's wishes for breakfast in bed later on on the morning of June 17. And her last thoughts are of her husband. Above all, even if Bloom does lose Molly to Boylan, Bloom finds comfort in knowing that Blazes is only the "last term of a preceding series. . . ."

QUESTIONS FOR REVIEW

1. At the end of "Telemachus," Stephen decides to leave the Martello Tower. What factors lead to this decision?

2. In "Nestor," how do Mr. Deasy's views on women, history, Jews, and finances anticipate similar viewpoints of other characters in *Ulysses*? How do his ideas contribute to Joyce's satiric intent in the novel?

3. "Proteus" deals with change. What elements of Stephen's past must he come to terms with? What are his present options?

4. Show how "Calypso" portrays Bloom as a man who delights in the physical world.

5. Discuss how Joyce creates a dreamlike, soporific atmosphere in "The Lotus-Eaters." How does Bloom's relationship with Martha Clifford typify the tone of the episode?

6. Show in detail how "Hades" presents Bloom's estrangement from the Roman Catholic community of Dubliners, as well as his loneliness and his wit.

7. In "Aeolus," what views of Ireland are presented by the discussants in the newspaper office? How does Stephen's Parable of the Plums synthesize many of their ideas?

8. "The Lestrygonians" presents several pedestrian aspects of Dublin life. How does Bloom's point of view concerning these everyday happenings determine what the reader sees?

9. Discuss in detail Stephen's views concerning Shakespeare ("Scylla and Charybdis"). How are they influenced by his interlocutors? How do they reflect his own personality and problems?

10. Describe Joyce's use of illusions in "The Wandering Rocks." Also, how does the structure of mini-episodes contribute to the over-all form of *Ulysses*?

11. How do the musical allusions in "The Sirens" define the personalities of Bloom, Simon Dedalus, and the others in the episode?

12. How does Joyce create an ever-increasing atmosphere of gloom and menace in "The Cyclops"? What does the climactic confrontation of Bloom and the Citizen reveal about the two men?

13. How does the "marmalady" style of "Nausicaa" augment Joyce's purpose in the episode? Also, discuss his use of parallel motifs in "Nausicaa."

14. In "The Oxen of the Sun," Joyce parodies several historical periods in the development of the English language. What purpose is served by such satire? Explain in detail.

15. Discuss how the events in "Circe," on both a conscious and an unconscious level, serve as a catharsis — that is, a purgation for Bloom and Stephen.

16. What purpose do the yarns and other fabrications of "Eumaeus" serve? How do they reflect the major themes in *Ulysses*?

17. How does the catechetical question-and-answer format contribute to Joyce's conveying a sense of "infinity" and objectivity in "Ithaca"?

18. Discuss in detail the character of Molly Bloom as it is revealed in "Penelope."

SELECTED BIBLIOGRAPHY

ADAMS, ROBERT M. *Surface and Symbol: The Consistency of James Joyce's Ulysses.* New York: Oxford University Press, 1962.

ANDERSON, CHESTER G. *James Joyce and His World.* London: Thames and Hudson, 1967.

BENSTOCK, SHARI, AND BERNARD BENSTOCK. *Who's He When He's at Home: A James Joyce Directory.* Urbana, Chicago: University of Illinois Press, 1980.

BLAMIRES, HARRY. *The Bloomsday Book: A Guide Through Joyce's Ulysses.* London: Methuen & Co., Ltd., 1966.

BOWEN, ZACK. *Musical Allusions in the Works of James Joyce: Early Poetry Through Ulysses.* Albany: S.U.N.Y. Press, 1974.

BOYLE, ROBERT, S. J. *James Joyce's Pauline Vision: A Catholic Exposition.* Carbondale: Southern Illinois University Press; London: Feffer, 1978.

BUDGEN, FRANK S. C. *James Joyce and the Making of Ulysses, and Other Writings.* Introd. Clive Hart. London: Oxford University Press, 1972. [Facsim. Rpt. of 1st Ed.: London: Grayson, 1934].

DEMING, ROBERT H. *A Bibliography of James Joyce Studies.* Rev. and Enl., 2nd. ed. Reference Publications in Literature. Boston: G. K. Hall, 1977.

———. *James Joyce: The Critical Heritage.* London: Routledge & K. Paul; New York: Barnes & Noble, 1970.

DRIVER, CLIVE, ed. *James Joyce's Ulysses: A Facsimile of the Manuscript.* 2 vols. New York: Octagon, 1976.

ELLMANN, RICHARD. *James Joyce.* New York: Oxford University Press, 1959.

————, ed. *Selected Letters of James Joyce.* New York: Viking, 1975.

————. *Ulysses on the Liffey.* New York: Oxford University Press; London: Faber, 1972.

FRENCH, MARILYN. *The Book as World: James Joyce's Ulysses.* Cambridge: Harvard University Press, 1976.

GIFFORD, DON, WITH ROBERT J. SEIDMAN. *Notes for Joyce: An Annotation of James Joyce's Ulysses.* New York: E.P. Dutton & Co., Inc., 1974.

GILBERT, STUART. *James Joyce's Ulysses.* 2nd. ed., revised. New York: Vintage Books, 1952. [First published 1930.]

GOLDBERG, S. L. *The Classical Temper: A Study of James Joyce's Ulysses.* London: Chatto & Windus; New York: Barnes & Noble, 1961.

GRODEN, MICHAEL. *Ulysses in Progress.* Princeton: Princeton University Press, 1977.

HART, CLIVE. *James Joyce's Ulysses.* University Park: Penn State University Press; Sydney: Sydney University Press; London: Methuen, 1968.

HART, CLIVE, AND DAVID HAYMAN. *James Joyce's Ulysses: Critical Essays.* Berkeley: University of California Press, 1974.

HART, CLIVE, AND LEO KNUTH. *A Topographical Guide to James Joyce's Ulysses.* 2 vols. Colchester, England: Wake Newslitter, 1975.

HAYMAN, DAVID. *Ulysses: The Mechanics of Meaning.* Englewood Cliffs, N. J.: Prentice-Hall, 1970.

HENKE, SUZETTE A. *Joyce's Moraculous Sindbook: A Study of Ulysses.* Columbus: Ohio State University Press, 1978.

HERRING, PHILLIP F., ed. *Joyce's Notes and Early Drafts for Ulysses: Selections from the Buffalo Collection.* Charlottesville: University of Virginia Press, 1975.

————, ed. *Joyce's Ulysses Notesheets in the British Museum.* Charlottesville: University of Virginia Press, for the Bibliographic Society, 1972.

HODGART, MATTHEW J. C., AND MABEL P. WORTHINGTON. *Song in the Works of James Joyce.* New York: Columbia University Press, for Temple University Publications, 1959.

KAIN, RICHARD M. *Fabulous Voyager: James Joyce's Ulysses.* Chicago: University of Chicago Press, 1947.

KENNER, HUGH. *Dublin's Joyce.* Bloomington: Indiana University Press, 1956.

KOPPER, EDWARD A., JR., ed. *James Joyce: New Glances.* Modern British Literature Monograph Series, 2. Butler, Pa.: Edward A. Kopper, Jr., 1980.

LEVIN, HARRY. *James Joyce: A Critical Introduction.* Rev. and Augm. Ed. New York: New Directions, 1960.

LITZ, A. WALTON. *The Art of James Joyce: Method and Design in Ulysses and Finnegans Wake.* London and New York: Oxford University Press, 1961.

————. *James Joyce.* Twayne's English Authors Series, 31. New York: Twayne, 1966.

MOSELY, VIRGINIA D. *Joyce and the Bible.* DeKalb: Northern Illinois University Press, 1967.

NOON, WILLIAM T. *Joyce and Aquinas.* Yale Studies in English, vol. 133. New Haven: Yale University Press, 1957.

RALEIGH, JOHN HENRY. *The Chronicle of Leopold and Molly Bloom: Ulysses as Narrative.* Berkeley: University of California Press, 1977.

SCHUTTE, WILLIAM M. *Joyce and Shakespeare: A Study in the Meaning of Ulysses.* Yale Studies in English, vol. 134. New Haven: Yale University Press, 1957.

SEIDEL, MICHAEL. *Epic Geography: James Joyce's Ulysses.* (Maps drawn by Thomas Crawford.) Princeton: Princeton University Press, 1976.

SHECHNER, MARK. *Joyce in Nighttown: A Psychoanalytic Inquiry into Ulysses.* Berkeley: University of California Press, 1974.

STALEY, THOMAS F., AND BERNARD BENSTOCK, eds. *Approaches to Ulysses: Ten Essays*. Pittsburgh: University of Pittsburgh Press, 1970.

STEINBERG, ERWIN R. *The Stream of Consciousness and Beyond in Ulysses*. Pittsburgh: University of Pittsburgh Press, 1973.

SULTAN, STANLEY. *The Argument of Ulysses*. Columbus: Ohio State University Press, 1964.

THORNTON, WELDON. *Allusions in Ulysses: An Annotated List*. Chapel Hill: University of North Carolina Press, 1968.

TINDALL, WILLIAM YORK. *The Joyce Country*. University Park: Penn State University Press, 1960.

_____. *A Reader's Guide to James Joyce*. New York: Noonday Press, 1959.

NOTES